Whip Up MINI QUILTS

Whip Up MINI QUILTS

PATTERNS AND HOW-TO
for MORE THAN 20
CONTEMPORARY SMALL QUILTS

by KATHREEN RICKETSON
photographs by LEIGH BEISCH

CHRONICLE BOOKS
SAN FRANCISCO

Library of Congress Cataloging-in-Publication Data:
Ricketson, Kathreen.
  Whip up mini quilts : patterns and how-to for more
than 20 contemporary small quilts / by Kathreen
Ricketson.
    p. cm.
  Includes index.
  ISBN 978-0-8118-6873-0   4339 1008 5/10
1. Quilting—Patterns. 2. Miniature quilts. I. Title.

TT835.R5365 2010
746.46'041--DC22

2009026021

Printed in China
Designed by Tracy Sunrize Johnson.
Photo styling by Sara Slavin.
Typesetting by Blue Friday.

10 9 8 7 6 5 4 3 2 1

Chronicle Books
680 Second Street
San Francisco, California 94107
www.chroniclebooks.com

Contents

INTRODUCTION 6
Small quilts 7
How to use this book 8
Short history of the quilt 8

SELECTING YOUR FABRICS 11
Color 11
Working with fabric 12

TOOLS 14
Sewing machine 14
Basic tools 16
Extras 16
Products 18
Storage ideas for your sewing supplies 19
On-the-go sewing kit 19

MAKING THE QUILT TOP 20
Quilt blocks and piecing 20

APPLIQUÉ 23
Reverse appliqué 25

OTHER DECORATIVE ELEMENTS 25
Stenciling 26
Dyeing fabric 26

STITCH DICTIONARY 29
Essential hand sewing stitches 29
Essential embroidery stitches 30

PREPARING FOR QUILTING 33
Backing 33
Batting 33
Basting 34

QUILTING 36
Hand quilting 36
Machine quilting 37
Binding 39

DISPLAYING AND CARING FOR YOUR QUILT 45
Hanging your quilt 45
Signing and labeling quilts 46
Caring for quilts 46

PROJECTS

Romantic 47
Pensive Pansy Photo Quilt 48
English Flower Garden Quilt 52
Follow Your Heart Art Quilt 56

Playful 61
Loopy Quilt 62
T-R-E-G-R-! Map Quilt 66
Circus Quilt 70
Road Transport Quilted Pillow 76

Modern Folk 81
Warbler Quilt 82
Blackbird at My Window ("Cheeky Blackbird") 86
Grasshopper in My Garden 90
A Little Birdie Told Me 96

Modern Elegance 101
Shibori Sampler 102
Blattwerk 106
Power-line Sky 110
Concentric Circles 114

Geometric 119
Cheater's ("Aunty Cookie") Quilt 120
Modern Geometric Quilt 124
Constellations Quilt 128

Punk, Pop, and Politics 131
Granny's Delight 132
1984 ("Pegasus Rainbow") Quilt 136
Target Pillow 142
Two Heads Are Better than One 146

Memories and Storytelling 151
Keepsake Quilt 152
Imagine 156

GLOSSARY *of* **TERMS** 162

SEWING *and* **QUILTING RESOURCES GUIDE** 166

DESIGNER BIOS 170

INDEX 174

ACKNOWLEDGMENTS 176

Introduction

My beloved Nanna was an incredible woman with amazing skills and resilience. She was my crafting hero and appreciated not only the process of creating but also the value and frugality of repurposing things. I used to laugh when my grandmother and her sister would collect bread bags and crochet them into coat hanger covers. But my grandmother reminded me that by making things she could have luxuries she could never afford otherwise.

My life is much easier than my grandmother's ever was. I craft for pleasure rather than necessity (with more gadgets to help me out). I choose to make my children's clothing, even though it would be more convenient (and cheaper) to buy them from a department store (those store-bought clothes feel impersonal and disposable to me). As I juggle my various roles as career woman, mother, and wife, I make sure to squeeze in a little time to create; it helps me get back to being me. Just like it was for my grandmother and so many other women, crafting is my time to dream and think and imagine.

For me, handcraft is not just about making more stuff. It is about giving a part of myself—the payoff is the satisfaction of giving—and about telling stories and expressing opinions. When I started a personal blog a few years ago, I had just had my second baby and finished five years at university. Suddenly I found myself a stay-at-home mother, cut off from my previous life as an artist, and without inspiration. Surprisingly, I found my creative energy again through the world of online craft blogs (who knew?). I discovered new designers, artists, makers, and a ton of amazing online resources.

I couldn't believe that all this information was at my fingertips. I soon started WhipUp.net: Handcraft in a Hectic World. It really is a hectic world that we modern women live in: working, mothering, running a house, and all the time trying to keep our own creative space going. That is what WhipUp is about—bringing together creative people and providing a space for them to share their stories, showcase their crafts, and offer up resources, ideas, and information.

Crafting for me, and many others, is about taking more control of your life. In this time of fast technological advancements, economic uncertainty, and the need for greater environmental awareness, being able to choose the materials used in your home and on your body is increasingly important. "Upcycle" and "re-fashion" are the new buzzwords in crafting today, and you'll see their influence in this book, in projects that show you how to use what you already have. Just like the women in the 1930s who recycled feed sacks for their sewing projects, women today are deconstructing clothing, felting old moth-eaten sweaters, and crocheting plastic shopping bags. They are taking control of how they use resources and live on this planet.

When I am crafting, both the process and the project drive me; I often experiment with new materials, techniques, and ideas. This is how I work when making quilts. With a deep respect for traditional quilt designs, but without the patience or time to give them the care they need, I prefer to improvise and experiment, and making small quilts is a perfect way for me to do just that.

This book of small quilts brings together just a handful of the amazing artists, makers, and designers I have either connected with through the handcraft blog scene or discovered by seeing their work online. These twenty-four makers, including myself, come from all over the world: Japan, Australia, Finland, England, and the United States. I have chosen these people to contribute to this book because of how they've inspired me. I'm confident that their work will inspire you, too.

SMALL QUILTS

I love the satisfaction of finishing a quilt and seeing my children snuggle up under it while I read them a bedtime story, but finishing a full-size quilt is a big project. This is why making a small quilt, or mini quilt, is so delicious—it's an achievable weekend project for any level of quilter; you can try out your new ideas and designs and see them through to fruition almost the next day!

I see today's mini quilt as a modern take on the traditional sampler quilt, which was used as a teaching tool for young quilters. Similarly, in the early nineteenth century, doll quilts were used to teach girls the first steps in sewing and quilt making. Every girl was expected to learn to sew, and many began by sewing for their dolls. These doll quilts, and other small quilts made for babies and children, were miniature copies of full-size designs. Only later in the century, when the concept of childhood took on a greater importance, were quilts designed specifically for children. These quilts began to reflect children's interests, depicting stories and animals for the purpose of educating. In addition, doll quilts were no longer made only by young girls; suddenly,

mothers, aunts, and grandmothers were making sweet little quilts with fine stitching and designs for the little girls in their lives.

Small quilts have come a long way from their beginnings as learning tools and sentimental gifts. Mini quilts, for me and for many other contemporary and

traditional makers, present an incredible medium with which to play with fabric, color, design, ideas, and techniques. They allow the maker to express their creativity, and they can easily become works of modern art.

HOW TO USE THIS BOOK

Consider this book a primer for making small quilts. You'll find a wide range of quilt designs from talented makers, organized by style, with quilt patterns ranging from super-simple to quite tricky. For the most part, the instructions for each quilt will help you replicate it exactly, but occasionally you'll find suggestions for improvising your own version. Just as you would with a food recipe, it is usually a good idea to follow the instructions exactly the first time and then play around with them to suit your personal tastes after that.

If you have never made a quilt before and have only basic sewing skills, then this book is the perfect way for you to build up your sewing knowledge. Start with the easy quilts and slowly work your way up to the medium-level quilts, leaving the tricky ones for last. If you already have strong sewing and quilting skills, then you can head straight to some of the medium-level and trickier projects. There are plenty of new techniques and original designs in here to keep you inspired. Plus two more patterns are offered at www.chroniclebooks.com/miniquilts.

You can use the mini quilts you create (and, believe me, you will have quite a few once you get started) in all sorts of ways: as a bevy of doll quilts for all the little girls in your life, to cover a collection of cushions in your living room, or as lovely place mats to dress up your table. Or, create a beautiful display of all of your mini quilts to hang on your wall.

SHORT HISTORY OF THE QUILT

The materials, design, and techniques used in each and every quilt tell a story about the maker and the community that he or she came from. Every community and every culture has its own textile traditions that reflect the makers' way of life. In cultures all over the world, patchwork and quilting are part of textile traditions; it seems no one can resist the temptation to use up bits of cloth while beautifying one's surroundings.

Patchwork and quilting are both ancient arts, over a thousand years old, with the earliest examples coming from Egypt. Quilting was brought to Europe via the Saracens eight hundred years ago, when quilted armor was worn during the crusades. Appliqué and patchwork have been used for a thousand years by Central Asian nomadic tribes to make saddle blankets and tents, and patchwork banners and bags have been found in Buddhist monks' caves dating from the ninth century.

Patchwork and appliqué designs have important meanings in every culture. In some religious communities, patchwork has symbolized modesty and piety, while in others it was a symbol of wealth and desirability; it was sometimes used to ward off demons, tell stories, and as integral parts of ceremonial traditions.

Quilting, as we know it in Western cultures today, has its roots in Europe, with ornate appliqué and quilting being used in the church and by royalty during the sixteenth and seventeenth centuries. While patchwork was a practical way for the common classes to recycle or extend the life of old clothing, quilting was a pastime only the wealthy could afford.

Americans have made patchwork quilting their own and today it is acknowledged to be a uniquely American form of folk art. It was popularized in the mid-nineteenth century, with various religious communities and regions each contributing their own unique styles. The Amish made beautifully austere quilts from dark woolen fabrics, for example, and people brought to America as slaves from Africa brought their textile heritage with them and used quilting as a medium for telling stories and documenting their lives, improvising with fabrics at hand.

Early Colonial American quilts, made by those wealthy enough to have leisure time, consisted of a whole cloth, with quilting as the only decoration, or *broderie perse*, where motifs were appliquéd onto the cloth before quilting. In contrast, pioneer women made nonquilted patchwork coverlets from worn-out men's woolen pants and jackets, often stuffing them with raw wool for added warmth.

It was not until the growth of the textile industry in the mid-1800s increased the availability of commercial fabric that quilt making became a common way for American women to express their creativity, decorate their homes, and keep their families warm. It also became a way for women to connect with each other. They gathered at quilting bees and shared block patterns, first through sampler quilts and then, in the late 1800s and early 1900s, through published patterns in catalogs and magazines.

Quilts were also a way for women to express their political convictions. In fact, quilt making was one of the earliest forms of political protest for women in America. In the 1830s when abolitionists pushed for antislavery laws, women held handcraft fairs to raise money and awareness, and during the Civil War, Northern women made protest quilts by the thousands.

After the Civil War, the lavish "crazy quilts" of the Victorian era became popular among the wealthy. And the "charm quilt," in which no two patches are the same, started a fabric swatch-swapping obsession among quilt-magazine readers. Sentimentality drove the popularity of "album quilts," with quilt blocks and treasured fabrics swapped through the mail among friends across the country.

Toward the end of the nineteenth century, quilts began to be seen as old-fashioned, and, with more manufactured linens for the home becoming available, quilt making fell out of favor. However, in the country, quilt making was not forgotten, and the most popular of American quilt designs emerged: the "log cabin quilt."

The 1920s saw a quilt-making revival among young women. It was a prosperous time in America, and new fabrics and new styles—fresh romantic designs and appliqué and embroidery—were particularly popular. The sewing machine had become a common household appliance, and patterns were readily available through magazine subscriptions, so creating patchwork designs was faster than ever before.

Quilting continued to thrive during the Depression of the 1930s, since making a quilt was an inexpensive way a woman could express her creativity (and keep her family warm) by using materials she had on hand. This was a time of innovation in quilt making, when the production of cheap printed cotton fabric, improved dye technologies, and the influence of the Art Deco movement meant that quilts became more colorful and the designs more stylized. Around this time there was interest in whimsical designs for children, the most popular being "sunbonnet Sue." In addition, new quilt block designs, such as "Dresden plate" and "double wedding ring" were available as kits. Scrap quilts were also popular; yo-yo coverlets and hexagon paper pieced mosaic quilts were perfect uses for fabric scraps. "Grandmother's flower garden," with its simplicity and repeated hexagon design, became the most popular quilt design of this era.

However, the biggest innovation during the Depression was the reuse of the humble feed sack. This had, in fact, been going on since the beginning of the century but by the 1930s, "feed sack mania" was at an all-time high, and feed sack manufacturers began printing the sacks with different designs and patterns. These became very popular with quilt makers—and many of these designs are still being printed as reproduction vintage fabrics.

During World War II, quilting mostly went out of fashion, since many women had to go to work and no longer had time for sewing. In rural areas, however, the practicality of quilting didn't lessen; quilt making was a comfort that helped reduce the isolation and loneliness of rural life. Country quilters took quilt making in new directions and were the innovators during this time, incorporating the "crazy quilt" scrap style but using more practical fabrics to make "country-style" quilts with no particular pattern. Today, we call quilts made in this style "improvised pieced quilts."

The 1970s saw the emergence of another quilt revival. The 1971 exhibition titled Abstract Design in American Quilts at New York's Whitney Museum of American Art, which portrayed quilts as art objects, sparked a renewed interest in quilts and brought Amish quilts to the attention of the public. The simple beauty of Amish quilting became a source of inspiration for modern quilters.

Today, crafters connect with each other through blogs, forums, and Web sites, resulting in a huge exchange of ideas across cultures. In addition, the Japanese Zakka craze for simplicity of design and natural materials, and the recent interest in the bold, improvised quilts made by the women of Gee's Bend, Alabama, have inspired a new generation of quilters.

Quilting today is no longer a necessity, but it remains a powerful way to connect with others, to show love for your family, to bring color and personal style into your home, and to express your political convictions. There have been many quilting revivals and recessions throughout the years, but, with each revival, quilting comes back bigger and better, bringing with it innovation and inspiration—new fabrics, designs, patterns, and techniques—and also a deep appreciation of quilting history, traditional design, and the women innovators from the past.

Selecting Your Fabrics

Choosing fabric is such a personal process. Some quilters prefer unbleached, natural, or hand-dyed fabric; others love commercial prints and crisp cottons, while still others prefer vintage fabrics, faded linens, and delicate silks. Whatever your preference, just make sure that the fabric you select for your project is suitable for its eventual use. If you are planning to turn your mini quilt into a place mat for your dining table, then choose sturdy, machine-washable fabrics. However, if your mini quilt will be displayed in a frame on the wall, then feel free to use more of your precious delicates.

When I buy fabric I tend to follow my instincts. If I don't have a particular plan for the fabric, I just buy a small amount, say ¼ or ½ yard (or meter) of a more expensive fabric or a couple of yards/meters of bargain fabric. If I find fabric in a charity shop or thrift store, then I buy it if I absolutely love it or if I know I will use it. Because the projects in this book are for mini quilts, you won't need much fabric, half a yard or meter at most, and most of this will be in smaller pieces. You will most likely have the fabric you need already; if not, then you need only purchase a small amount (see each project for yardage specifications).

Quite a few of the projects in this book recommend vintage fabrics or fabric pieces salvaged from clothing or table linens. Reusing fabric in this way adds charm and a personal touch to your projects. My advice is to collect these treasures bit by bit as you see them. Garage sales, thrift stores, and church and school rummage sales are wonderful places to search out bargain fabrics. Keep an eye out for old clothing with interesting buttons, lace, or edgings. Also, don't dismiss tablecloths, tea towels, aprons, and bed linens as sources of interesting materials.

COLOR

Color is also very personal, and most people know what they do and don't like. But if you are in a color rut and find yourself going for the same color combinations every time, then you might want to step out of your comfort zone every now and again. I naturally gravitate to warm tones—browns, reds, and pinks—but my daughter recently persuaded me to include yellow and black in my designs, with interesting results.

There are many places to get inspiration for new color combinations. Use the good ol' color wheel for tried-and-true combinations. (Read up a little on color theory if you are unfamiliar with the color wheel.) You can also take your cue from the colors that appear in a patterned fabric that you love, or you can take a walk around your garden or a park and pick out the colors of your favorite leaves and flowers.

A fun but slightly more involved method, if you have access to a computer and photo-editing software, is to "pixelate" a colorful digital photo. Zoom in until all you can see are pixels, or blocks of color, and use these as inspiration for your fabrics. There are also some online color-palette-generating tools, which are fun to play with if you're stuck (see page 168 for a list of these tools).

WORKING WITH FABRIC

Over the years I have built up quite a collection of fabrics and love to sort through them to find just the right thing for each project. However, storing them properly is important, not only for the good of the fabric but also so you can lay your hands on just what you want when you want it. In an ideal world, I would store my fabric folded in a place where air can circulate while keeping the fabrics free of dust. However, lack of shelf space means I store most of my fabric, clearly labeled, in plastic wheelie boxes.

WASHING FABRIC

I recommend washing your fabric before starting a project. Some people go as far as to wash, dry, and fold their fabric immediately after they buy it so they don't have to worry about it later when they are starting their projects. If, like me, you are not that organized, you will probably only prewash your fabrics when absolutely necessary—such as when the colors might bleed. I always prewash red and dark-colored fabrics by hand with gentle laundry soap until the water runs clear and then pop the pieces in the dryer (this takes care of any shrinkage issues as well). I only wash other fabrics if I have the time (I admit to laziness here). If you are worried about your fabric shrinking or colors running, or if you want to remove any chemicals in the fabric, then please do prewash.

When you are making a quilt and you want that old-fashioned wrinkled look, you may want to hold off on washing until after you have finished making it. Just make sure you don't use any fabrics that will bleed onto the surrounding fabrics.

Washing vintage fabrics is a whole other story. (Note that I am not talking about valuable antique linens and quilts here; these would require a different approach.) Vintage fabrics are often delicate, may have mold spots or rust stains, and require special treatment. Use old-fashioned pure vegetable soap flakes to gently hand wash and then hang on a line to air dry. For stubborn rust stains, try a paste of vinegar and salt. To remove mold spots, wash in a salt-and-lemon-juice solution: make a paste with ¼ cup/55 g salt and ¼ cup/60 ml lemon juice, mix with a pint of warm water, rub into the stain, and let dry in the sun for a few hours before washing out. Store vintage fabrics carefully rolled, not folded (since they are more susceptible to developing permanent creases), in an airing cupboard if you have one, or in a dust-free, dry area.

PRESSING FABRIC

A steam iron for pressing fabric while sewing is absolutely essential. Pressing seams as you go not only makes for easier sewing but also gives a professional finish with a lovely, crisp seam line. There is an art to proper pressing: it is important to lift the iron and press down rather than moving and sliding; the latter can stretch the fabric out of shape.

Traditionally, seams are pressed open in dressmaking and to one side on patchwork, usually toward the darker fabric. Though I like to press my seams open on patchwork, professional quilters usually frown upon this. But there is a time and place for utilizing both methods; just make sure you stay consistent across your quilt.

Whether you choose to press your seams open or to the side depends upon the needs of each project.

Pressing seams to one side, a tradition left over from the time when seams were hand sewn, gives added durability. When you are pressing seams open, there is a chance that you may end up with a gap in the seam line, which can leave it vulnerable to "bearding," in which the batting leaks through into the quilt top. This won't happen when you are pressing seams to one side, and it will rarely occur with machine-sewn patches. Another advantage of pressing toward the dark side is that you will not see the darker fabric through the lighter fabric.

On the other hand, pressing seams open helps the quilt top to lie flat. If you are piecing a complex design, with pieces going in opposite directions and multiple seams coming together, such as a star pattern, then pressing the seams open is essential. This will result in a much flatter block, preventing seams from becoming bulky and twisted, and making it a whole lot easier to quilt across seam lines. You will find that the designers in this book all have personal preferences and recommendations for pressing seams.

Fabric is all about personal choice. Be guided by what you love and by what turns you on.

Tools

For the projects in this book, you only really need a sewing machine, a bit of space where you can set yourself up, and a basic sewing kit. Down the road you may want to expand your kit to include some extras, but I will only be discussing those tools that are relevant to quilting and the simple embroidery and appliqué techniques used in the quilts in this book.

Save yourself time by keeping your tools and sewing area organized. Begin by finding a sewing box, basket, or caddy for your supplies. Any container with small compartments will work, such as a builder's toolbox or fisherman's tackle box. As you build up your tool kit, you can move your sewing tools into a larger set of drawers or compartments.

SEWING MACHINE

Invest in a good sewing machine. It doesn't need to be fancy, but it should be sturdy (one that has some weight to it, has metal parts, and doesn't vibrate all over the table when you have your pedal to the metal). A secondhand machine can be excellent, but be sure to test it before buying, and get it serviced before you start using it. Another good idea is to borrow a sewing machine from a friend, so you can learn about what you want or don't want in a machine before investing in one.

All sewing machines will do the basic stitches. You might also want to look out for extras such as blanket stitch and buttonholes. Also make sure that you can lower the feed dogs (see facing page); this is essential if you are doing any type of freestyle sewing such as embroidery or quilting.

It is important to care for your machine. Take it in for a regular service just as you would your car and learn how to clean it properly. Use the small tool kit (and manual) that comes with your machine (usually a small screwdriver, lint brush, sewing machine oil, and tweezers) to maintain it, and change the needle before each new project. Make sure to keep your sewing machine manual handy. Doing these small tasks will ensure that your machine remains in tiptop shape and runs like a dream.

PRESSER FEET

A presser foot helps to guide the fabric under the needle and over the throat plate. There are many different feet available for different purposes; your machine should come with a few basic feet, such as a zipper foot, buttonhole foot, and multipurpose foot.

A few extra feet that are handy for the projects in this book include the following:

• A walking foot is useful for sewing several layers of fabric; it "walks" the fabric so that the bottom layer of fabric moves at the same speed as the top. Use this foot when quilting straight lines or sewing binding.

• An embroidery or darning foot is used for free-motion sewing such as stipple quilting or embroidery. Use this foot when lowering the feed dogs on your machine.

• A ¼-in/6-mm presser foot is useful when accurate seams are important.

FEED DOGS

The feed dogs on your sewing machine are those metal teeth that come up through the throat plate and pull the fabric along in small incremental movements, controlling the speed of the fabric and the length of the stitches. When you lower these, you have freedom to move the fabric in any direction. Quite a few projects in this book require you to be able to lower the feed dogs on your machine. Consult your manual for instructions on how to lower the feed dogs. Newer machines have a simple lever or setting, but if yours is an old but sturdy machine, you may need to get out the tiny screwdriver in your tool kit and remove the feed dogs manually.

BEFORE YOU START:

Quick sewing machine checklist

Bobbins

If you are working on a large project, it's a good idea to fill a few bobbins with the correct thread so you don't have to stop and start (especially when you are machine quilting).

Lighting and comfort

Most machines come with a small light above the presser foot, but you will need additional lighting for working. Consider adding a good desk lamp or track lights to your work area. Make sure your work surface and chair are at a comfortable height in order to prevent bad posture and avoid a strained back.

Needles

Make sure you have spare sewing machine needles on hand. It's terribly frustrating to have your last needle break while you are in the middle of a project. Ensure that the needles you do have are suitable for the job—you should keep a supply of universal needles and some for specialized sewing, such as sharps for knit fabrics and heavy-duty needles for thick and industrial-weight fabrics.

Tension check

The upper and lower tensions must be balanced to produce a perfect stitch. If you are unsure about how to measure the tension, check your user manual. Generally, if the loops of the bobbin thread show on the top side of the seam, then you need to lessen the tension; if the loops of the spool thread show on the underside of the seam, then you need to increase the tension.

Thread

High-quality thread is important to keep your machine running smoothly. Cheap thread will break easily and leave behind a lot of lint in your bobbin tray. You should generally match your thread material with that of the fabric—and use the same thread in the bobbin as in the spool. Specific types of thread come with particular benefits; for example, thread that is 100 percent cotton is best used on natural fiber fabrics, hand-quilting thread has a waxy coating to prevent tangles, and basting thread is lightweight, allowing you to break it easily when removing the basting stitches.

Tools to have handy

Pins and a pincushion, scissors for cutting thread, and a seam ripper are essential to have by your side so you don't have to keep getting up to look for things as you sew.

BASIC TOOLS

When sewing the projects in this book, or doing any basic sewing task, you'll need a few essential tools:

HAND-SEWING NEEDLES IN A VARIETY OF SIZES AND TYPES

Using the correct needle for the job saves time, saves your fabric, and keeps you from swearing rather a lot while you work. Keep sharps for all-purpose sewing, embroidery needles that have a larger eye to take decorative threads, and quilting needles.

IRON

An iron is the key to creating professional-looking projects; it enables you to make neat seams. Remember to press, not glide, to prevent any stretching of fabric. An ironing board is also useful, but if you don't have one you can lay out a towel or thick fabric onto a heat-proof table or workbench for pressing.

PINCUSHION

This is a small cushion that is used for holding pins. Pincushions can be made into all sorts of imaginative shapes, and stuffed with wool or pillow stuffing. You can make an extra pin-sharpening cushion by stuffing it with steel wool. Magnetic pin trays are handy, but I find them annoying, since the pins all stick together. For your on-the-go kit, a wrist pincushion is perfect.

PINS

Long, sharp steel pins with round glass heads work well for quilting projects. Dull pins can damage fabrics, so keep your pins sharp by occasionally using an emery pincushion, available at sewing and craft supply stores.

SCISSORS

You will need three basic types of scissors: small, sharp scissors perfect for clipping seams and precision cutting; a really good pair of fabric scissors that you will use for fabric only (buy the best ones you can afford and have them sharpened regularly); and another pair of utility scissors, which can be used for paper and miscellaneous cutting.

SEAM RIPPER

This is a small tool with a pointed tip, a small curved blade, and a tiny rubber ball that helps prevent the fabric from ripping. Use it for undoing stitches.

TAPE MEASURE

Choose a flexible one that you can roll up.

EXTRAS

Each of the projects in this book comes with a list of items that are needed or just useful for completing that project. Many of these items are recommended for multiple projects and are useful additions to your sewing tool kit.

BEESWAX

Beeswax is a lovely little extra to have to rub over the thread and needle when hand quilting. It strengthens the thread and helps reduce tangling.

BIAS TAPE MAKER

Feed your strips of fabric through this little metal gadget and, as the folded tape comes out the other side, press with a hot iron to make single-fold binding tape. These come in different widths and speed up the task of making binding.

CARBON PAPER

Use carbon paper for tracing embroidery designs onto fabric.

CLEAR ACRYLIC QUILTING RULER

A quilting ruler is transparent, has a wide surface, and has imperial and metric measurements. This type of ruler is essential for accurate cutting, ensuring nice straight lines when you are cutting fabric with your rotary cutter, and for squaring up edges.

CRAFT KNIFE

A craft knife, otherwise known as an X-Acto or Stanley knife, is a very useful tool for cutting out stencil and appliqué designs on paper or card.

DESIGN WALL

A design wall lets you arrange fabrics on a neutral background and see how they work together before you start sewing. You can make a design wall or board easily with a neutral-colored fabric, such as felt or cotton batting, to which other fabrics will cling.

EMBROIDERY OR HAND-QUILTING HOOP

An embroidery hoop is basically a pair of concentric circular rings made of wood or plastic that holds your fabric at an even tension while you sew. You place the fabric in between the rings and tighten with a screw.

FABRIC MARKING PEN, DISAPPEARING-INK PEN, AND TAILOR'S CHALK

Marks from fabric marking pens with water-soluble ink can be removed later with a damp sponge; disappearing-ink pens have air-dissolvable ink, and chalk pencil will simply rub off. Whatever type of fabric marker you use, be sure to test it first on a scrap of fabric to make sure it can be removed later.

LEATHER PUNCH

Use a leather punch for cutting holes in heavy-duty fabrics such as felt and leather.

MASKING TAPE

Masking tape is useful for marking edges and straight lines, and for holding fabric steady.

PAPER TO TRACE TEMPLATES

Tracing paper, brown paper, and craft papers are useful to have in your craft box.

PLASTIC COVER FOR YOUR WORKBENCH

A plastic-coated tablecloth will protect your work-bench when you are doing messy crafts such as painting or dyeing.

QUILTING GLOVES

Specialized quilting gloves help you to grip the fabric while you move it around, when you are doing free-motion quilting. Regular rubber gloves work just as well.

ROTARY CUTTER

A rotary cutter creates a smooth, even line when you are cutting fabric. The blades are extremely sharp, so use caution.

SAFETY PINS

You'll use safety pins at regular intervals for basting when machine quilting.

SELF-HEALING MAT

A cutting mat protects your work surface when you are using a craft knife or rotary cutter and has ruled lines to help guide you. Be sure to store your mat flat and not leave it in the sun, or it can warp.

THIMBLE

A thimble is used to protect your middle finger while you are hand sewing. Thimbles come in a variety of sizes and types. Try them on and select the one you find most comfortable.

PRODUCTS

There are many products on the market that can give you a little extra help on your projects. Make sure to read the manufacturer's directions carefully each time, with each product, and do a test on a scrap of material before using it on your project.

FABRIC GLUE

This glue temporarily holds fabric together until you sew.

FABRIC PAINT

Fabric paint is made especially for use on fabric; it usually needs to be heat set with a hot iron, after which it can be washed.

FREEZER PAPER

Freezer paper is a medium-weight white paper with a plastic coating on one side, generally used for wrapping food. When ironed, it clings to fabric, and, when removed, it leaves no residue. You'll find it in crafting applications for appliqué, templates, and stencils. You might use it as a guide for needle turning the seam allowance under for appliqué, for creating even circles for appliqué, for English paper piecing, as a backing to stabilize fabric so you can run it through your printer, as a tear-away stabilizer for embroidery, and as a stencil for fabric painting.

FRAY-CHECK SPRAY

This product is used for stopping raw fabric edges from fraying.

FUSIBLE INTERFACING OR STABILIZER

This product is ironed onto the **Wrong** side of the fabric and fuses to the fabric. It is used to add body and prevent stretching, and it comes in many weights, from very lightweight and soft to heavy-weight and stiff.

FUSIBLE WEB OR PAPER-BACKED ADHESIVE

This is a material that fuses fabric pieces together when pressed with a warm iron. It is generally used to position appliqué pieces on quilt tops.

IRON-ON TRANSFER PENCIL

A transfer pencil allows you to trace your design in reverse onto paper, and then flip the paper over and iron the design onto your fabric.

LAUNDRY STARCH

Laundry starch is available in a powdered or liquid concentrate; it can be mixed with water to the level of concentration you require. It is used as a spray to stiffen fabric during ironing, gives appliqué motifs a crisp edge when you are pressing them, and is easily washed out. Make your own laundry starch with cornstarch and water.

QUILT BASTING SPRAY

Some of the designers in this book recommend this as a quick and easy basting method. All products are different, so read the instructions carefully.

STORAGE IDEAS FOR YOUR SEWING SUPPLIES

My mother has inherited the most fantastic set of tall, narrow antique drawers—with compartments in each drawer—where she stores and organizes just about all of her little gadgets and sewing accoutrements. I am not lucky enough to have one of these; instead I use a small child's desk with cute little drawers as an extra worktable.

Stationery and storage containers are good for storing sewing gadgets, and paper envelopes are a great place to store patterns or templates. I like to use resealable plastic bags to sort everything from zippers to threads, and jam jars for leftover dye, buttons, ribbons, and other odd bits and pieces. I also use vintage cookie and tea tins to store my buttons—I love how they look!

ON-THE-GO SEWING KIT

A small sew-on-the-go kit is also a must. Set up a little sewing basket with a compartment for pins, and add small scissors, a wrist pincushion, a fold-up fabric needle holder, and a small resealable plastic bag for threads.

Making the Quilt Top

The quilt top is the showpiece of your quilt, where most of your handwork and design elements will appear. It is usually either pieced with patches of fabric sewn together in a design or appliquéd with pieces of fabric sewn on top of a background. Sometimes these elements are used together and combined with other techniques as well. You might use embroidery stitches, fabric painting, or any other fabric manipulation you like—there is no end to the creative possibilities.

QUILT BLOCKS AND PIECING

Quilts made up of blocks of pieced designs became popular around 1820, with different regions becoming known for their particular quilt block designs. Many of these designs were named for the region or for the story that inspired them.

Many patchwork blocks are made up of basic grid designs, with squares, triangles, and bars in a huge variety of combinations. If you want to know more about traditional block designs, check out a block design encyclopedia (see page 166).

Not many of the designs in this book use traditional block designs, but a few do, including the nine patch, log cabin, and others, described here.

NINE PATCH
The nine-patch design originated around the beginning of the nineteenth century and, due to its simplicity, was a common pattern used to make doll quilts and children's quilts.

The most basic nine-patch design is made up of three rows of three squares—making a block of nine squares. The Shibori Sampler on page 102 uses this basic design to showcase the Shibori dye samples. Blattwerk, the appliqué leaf quilt on page 106, uses the nine-patch design to showcase the unique wool leaves.

The nine-patch design is worth experimenting with, since it has so many different variations. Each of the nine squares can be divided further into smaller squares, triangles, and half circles.

FOUR PATCH

A four patch is a simple grid divided into quarters, which are themselves divided in a variety of ways, often in strips going in opposite directions or a variety of smaller squares and triangles. The Two Heads Are Better than One quilt on page 146 uses a traditional stair design, in which the squares are divided into two rectangles. This four-patch block is called either "winding stairway" or "endless stairs."

LOG CABIN

The log cabin design first made its appearance in America during the Civil War, and its popularity has endured because of the sense of warmth and home that it brings.

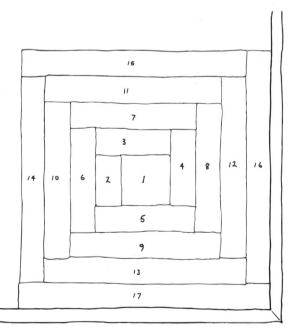

The center block is traditionally red to signify the hearth, with the logs overlapping each other and spiraling outward. The colors can be arranged in all kinds of ways. These different arrangements of light and dark colors have names such as "barn raising" and "courthouse steps." This block is used in the Follow Your Heart Art Quilt on page 56.

ENGLISH PAPER PIECING

The English paper piecing method uses paper templates to put together multisided pieces, usually hexagons, to form a honeycomb design. This method, as is suggested by its name, originated in England during the eighteenth century and may be the oldest pieced quilt pattern. This is a very time-consuming but sturdy way of piecing quilts. The most common design using this method is "Grandmother's flower garden," which is used as a feature in the English Flower Garden Quilt on page 52.

How to do it

To use this method, cut the templates out of paper first and then use them to cut the fabric, leaving ¼ in/6 mm all around, which is then folded over the template and basted down. Next, whipstitch the hexagons together at the edges, place them with **Right** sides facing, and whipstitch one side. Then open the fabric up and whipstitch in another hexagon.

IMPROVISATIONAL PIECING

Improvisational piecing is not a new idea. The free-form, cut and pieced quilts made with this method, in which pragmatism governed the improvisational use of materials and the design of blocks, were known as "country quilts." Quilts made by African Americans in the eighteenth century are said to be the earliest examples of American improvisational piecing. Amish quilt makers in the early 1900s sometimes improvised a central medallion, surrounded by a more formal framing. The Gee's Bend quilters have been quilting with this method since the early 1900s, using whatever materials were on hand to create stunning quilts in a folk art style.

This free-form method of piecing patchwork can be very liberating, since it enables you to follow your instinct. There are no precise blocks to cut or patterns to follow; it involves spontaneous and intuitive cutting and piecing and is a playful approach to working with fabric.

How to do it

One method is to start with a central idea, general shape, and piece of fabric. Sew a strip of fabric down one side of your central fabric (with **Right** sides together, as always). Press the seams, then take your scissors, or rotary cutter, ruler, and mat, and trim this central block. Trim it square (or on an angle), and then add another piece and press and trim. Keep working like this, adding pieces around the central block as you might do with a log cabin quilt.

- -

CURVED PIECING

A couple of the quilts in this book make use of curves, such as the Concentric Circles lap quilt on page 114 and the Power-line Sky quilt on page 110.

Piecing curves can seem quite daunting, but if you follow a few basic steps you will find that it really is rather simple.

How to do it

Whether you are using a pattern or creating a free-hand pieced curve, the principles are the same. On the paper pattern, draw registration marks through every seam line 1 to 2 in/2.5 to 5 cm apart (closer together on tighter curves); then transfer these marks, along with the pattern, onto the fabric using tailor's chalk. When cutting the fabric out, add a ¼-in/6-mm seam allowance. Place the two pieces with **Right** sides together, matching up the registration marks on the convex and concave curves, and pin into place. Sew along the seam line, removing the pins as you come to them. When you press, the seam will fall naturally toward the concave side. You may need to clip the seam allowance along the curves so the seam lays flat.

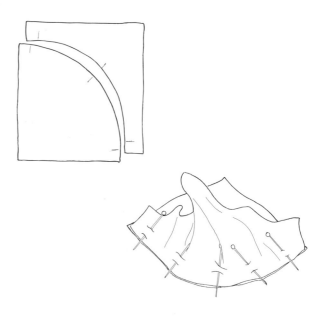

CHAIN PIECING

Chain piecing is an efficient way to speed things up when you are sewing multiples of the same pieces. Before you start, arrange your pieces in pairs, so they're ready to go. Only one of the quilts in this book, Two Heads Are Better than One (page 146), requires chain piecing. It's a good way to practice your skills before you embark on a large quilt.

How to do it

To use this method, feed fabric pairs through the sewing machine, one after another, with **Right** sides facing. Sew the seams without backstitching and without stopping to snip threads; the result will be a chain of sewn patches. Remove the chain of patches from the sewing machine and cut apart the sets. Press each set flat, and then get ready to attach your next piece onto these sets.

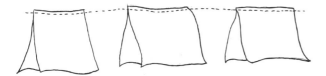

You can continue in this way until you have finished the blocks. Here's an important tip: since you are not reinforcing the seam at the beginning and end of each block by backstitching, you will need to use a slightly smaller stitch length than usual (size 2), so the seams don't unravel.

Appliqué is a very old technique used in art and craft all around the world. Examples have been found from as early as the eighteenth century.

Appliqué at its most basic is a simple technique with enormous design potential: it involves laying a design in fabric on top of a base fabric and stitching it around the edges.

As you can see from the variations within this book, there are lots of different ways you can use appliqué. You can leave the appliqué patches with a raw edge or you can turn the edges under. You can machine or hand sew these onto your background fabric using a simple or fancy stitch. You can make the patches by cutting freehand or by using templates. Use the method best suited to your skills and to the quilt design.

How to do it

Trace your design onto a paper template and cut it out. (You may want to label the template for later use.) Place the template **Right**-side up on the **Right** side of your appliqué fabric and pin in place; then trace around the edge with a fabric-marking pencil. (For an alternative way of tracing templates see the freezer paper method described on page 24.) Cut out your fabric appliqué pieces.

Next, decide which method you will use to attach the design onto your background fabric. The various methods (explained on the following pages) all have their pros and cons. Decide which one is right for your level of skill and your crafting style.

PINCH AND TURN

With this method, also known as "needle turn," you take your appliqué piece, with the seam line marked on the **Right** side of the fabric in tailor's chalk, and pin it into place onto your background. As you sew, turn the edges under to the marked line, using your needle to push the seam under, and use a blind hemming stitch (see page 29) to sew in place. This method takes a bit of practice. If you are trying it for the first time, try basting (see page 34) the appliqué piece in place to stop any movement and puckering.

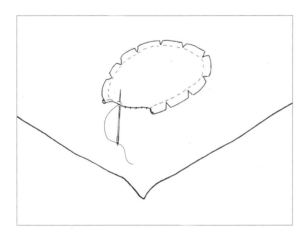

FREEZER PAPER APPLIQUÉ

Trace your design onto freezer paper (see page 18 for more about freezer paper) and iron it, wax-side down, onto the **Wrong** side of the fabric to hold it in place. Freezer paper will not leave any residue and can be reused. Cut around the template, leaving a ¼-in/6-mm seam allowance.

Next, dab some concentrated liquid starch (see page 19) using a cotton swab just on the seam allowance and fold it over the template edge (snip curves if necessary), and then press carefully with the tip of an iron to hold in place. Continue to press firmly with the hot iron, until you have a nice, crisp edge all around.

Remove the freezer paper template before attaching your appliqué piece to the background fabric. Pin, or use basting glue, to hold the piece in place while you sew.

FUSIBLE WEB OR PAPER-BACKED ADHESIVE

Use paper-backed fusible webbing to trace your templates. Don't cut them out just yet. Instead, first cut around them in a rough shape. Then iron the uncut templates, sticky-side down, onto the **Wrong** side of your fabric and cut the fabric out on the pencil line of your template.

Peel off the paper backing and place the fabric sticky-side down onto your background fabric. Adjust and arrange and then press into place with your hot iron. This is a great method for doing machine appliqué, raw edge appliqué, and more complex layered appliqué designs.

Depending upon the final look you want, you can choose from a variety of ways to sew around the edges of your appliqué pieces. For a subtle effect, you could hand sew the appliqué pieces with a blind hemming stitch. For a bolder look, you could use a more decorative stitch such as a running stitch or a blanket stitch. Alternatively, you may decide to machine stitch your appliqué in place. A regular zigzag is adequate for this purpose; however, you may like to use a more decorative stitch or a subtle blanket stitch if your machine allows. See Stitch Dictionary (page 29) for more details on the different hand stitches.

REVERSE APPLIQUÉ

In this technique, instead of applying an appliqué design to the top of the fabric background, you cut away the fabric background to reveal an under-lying fabric. The Constellations Quilt on page 128 and the Loopy Quilt on page 62 both use a variation of this method, while the Warbler Quilt (page 82) uses raw edge reverse appliqué in one small section.

How to do it

Lay your design templates onto your top layer of fabric and trace around them with a disappearing fabric marker. Then carefully cut out the designs, using small, sharp embroidery scissors. Lay this top piece (with the holes cut out) over a contrasting piece of fabric, both with **Right** sides facing up, pin into place, and stitch around the openings using a running stitch in a contrasting thread. If you don't want raw edges on your cut-out designs, then you will need to clip the edges of the cut-out designs and turn them under, just as you would using the pinch and turn method (see page 24), before sewing in place.

Quite a few of the quilts in this book incorporate elements beyond stitch and fabric for enhancement and finishing. In the Imagine quilt (page 156), a few tiny, discreet stenciled stars and swirls add to the whole flavor of the design. Others, such as the 1984 "Pegasus Rainbow" Quilt (page 136), and Granny's Delight (page 132), use stencils to add one of the major design elements to the quilt top.

Another way to embellish your quilt is to dye your fabric yourself. You'll see this technique in the Shibori Sampler (page 102) and in the English Flower Garden Quilt (page 52), where some hand-dyed fabric is used in the quilt background. A couple of the quilts in the book, Granny's Delight and the T-R-E-G-R-! Map Quilt, (page 66), use tea dyeing to add a slightly weathered and vintage look to the quilt.

Many of these design elements can be created in other ways. You could use the templates provided as embroidery designs or appliqué templates if stenciling is beyond you. Of course, tea dyeing can be simulated by using unbleached cotton or a beige-colored fabric, but it's fun to experiment with dyeing it yourself.

STENCILING

Using a stencil rather than drawing freehand allows you to copy a design exactly and ensure consistency in your repetitions. It's also fun to do!

How to do it

Create a negative of your motif by tracing your design onto acetate (clear heavy plastic), self-adhesive clear plastic (contact paper), medium-weight cardboard, or freezer paper. Then cut out the design carefully using a craft knife and a cutting mat, making sure to leave enough excess acetate, cardboard, or paper around your design in case you paint outside the edges.

Place your template carefully over your fabric. (Try it out first on a scrap of fabric before putting it directly onto your completed quilt top.)

If you are using freezer paper, iron it in place to prevent it from moving—the wax back will melt and allow it to temporarily stick to the fabric. If you are using contact paper, remove the sticky back and press onto your fabric. This can leave a residue, but it will wash out. Both of these methods prevent the paint from bleeding underneath the edges of the template. If you don't have these sticky papers handy, then taping your cardboard or acetate template carefully in place will suffice.

Put a little fabric paint onto a plate and dab your sponge or stencil brush into it; then paint it evenly over your design, filling in the negative space. You may need a couple of layers, but wait for it to dry in between the layers. Don't be tempted to apply the paint too heavily the first time, since it may bleed underneath the stencil and you won't have a crisp edge on your motif. After it dries you may need to heat set it with an iron; just check the fabric paint manufacturer's instructions.

DYEING FABRIC

When dyeing fabric, whether you are working with small samples or large pieces of fabric, you need to take the proper precautions. Always wear rubber gloves to protect your hands, put on an apron to protect your clothes, and use a plastic sheet to protect your work area. Depending on the type of dye you are using, you may also need eye protection and a gas mask. Be sure to read the directions. To learn more about dyeing, go to your local library or book shop and pick up a good book on the subject if you are interested in getting into it deeper.

Here are a few quick tips:

1. Have some clean, empty glass jars with lids handy to store leftover dye for another time.

2. Prewash your fabric before dyeing, since it may contain chemicals that can resist dye and prevent you from getting the best colors out of it.

3. Use white quilter's cotton to get the best results from your dye. Unbleached cotton can also be used but will affect the color outcome. Over-dyeing printed fabric offers some great design possibilities, as well.

4. Keep a notebook handy so you can take notes as you go. Then, if you really like your results, you can repeat them later.

TEA DYEING

Tea dyeing fabric gives it an antique and weathered look. It only works on natural fabrics and it may fade over time.

How to do it

Make a cup of strong black tea, using a couple of tea bags and letting them steep. Pour the tea into a wide pan and soak the fabric for a few minutes (up to 12 hours for a darker result) before gently wringing it out and lightly rinsing. Lay the fabric on a dark towel and heat set it with a hot iron. Alternatively, you can heat set it after it has dried, or pop it in a hot dryer to heat set.

- -

SHIBORI DYEING

Shibori is an ancient Japanese resist dye technique. The earliest examples found date to around 750 A.D.; however, there is written evidence of Shibori techniques being used in China and Japan as early as 418 A.D.

The wonderful thing about this method of dyeing is the element of chance that is involved. You'll never get the same results twice. Each step in the process is important to the end result; with practice and experimentation you will find what works best for you. There are hundreds of different Shibori designs, each with a specific name that describes the pattern created by combinations of shaping, securing, stitching, folding, clamping, and tying the cloth before it is dyed. The Shibori Sampler quilt (page 102) uses the "pleat, fold and clamp" method, but you may like to experiment with any of the methods described here.

One of the earliest, and possibly easiest, types of Shibori is "ring Shibori," where small circles are made by gathering a small bubble in the cloth and tying with thread around the base. For a more even ring design, you can place an object inside these bubbles, such as a smooth pebble or glass marble. Another very simple method of Shibori, commonly known as "tie-dye," involves many variations of binding and tying and can result in a huge range of effects.

"Stitched Shibori" gives great control over the finished design but is quite time consuming. The cloth is stitched using a small running stitch along a pre-drawn design and then gathered very tightly before dyeing.

"Pole-wrapping Shibori" is self-explanatory: the cloth is wrapped around a pole, usually on the diagonal, and then tied very tightly with thread up and down the pole, before being dunked in the dye bath.

With the "pleat, fold, and clamp" Shibori method, fabric is pleated or folded in different ways before being clamped in place. This is the method used to create the various samples used in the Shibori Sampler.

How to do it

Pleat and fold the fabric in different configurations and use an iron to give a crisp edge to your design.

Try folding your fabric samples in a grid design. First do an accordion fold along one edge, pressing as you go, and then pleat in the opposite direction, so you end up with a small square of fabric. Try this on the diagonal, or, as you take the folds in the opposite direction, fold them into triangles.

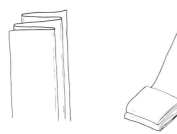

For a "resist" shape, fold the sample into triangles or squares and place a resist shape—such as a circle or small square of wood (experiment with other objects such as clothes pins or metal rings)—in the center of your folded fabric on each side. Clamp these resist shapes with hardware clamps or binder clips.

For a circle or flower design, fold the piece into quarters and press. Then bring the corners together and then together again to make a triangle, and clamp on the edges.

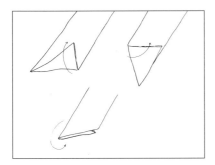

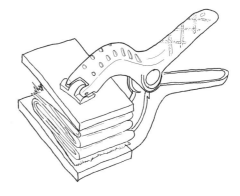

Try placing your folded fabric samples between two blocks of wood. You can use balsa wood from a craft store or any small wooden planks you might have around. Secure these blocks in place by tying them tightly with string, using clamps, or using binder clips.

To dye the folded fabric, dip the edges of the folds in the dye bath (follow the manufacturer's directions when preparing your dye bath) or dunk in the whole parcel. Wetting the folded parcel before dipping increases how much dye bleeds into the folds. It's up to you, so experiment with a few methods and with how long you leave it in the dye bath, though a few seconds is usually enough, since you won't be rinsing straightaway.

After you take the folded parcels out of your dye, carefully untie them right away. Do not rinse; instead, lay them out flat on your bench or table (covered with a plastic sheet) and leave for about 20 minutes. Then rinse in warm, soapy water, and once again in cold water until the water runs clear. Dry by either hanging them on a rack or running them briefly in the dryer before pressing and trimming.

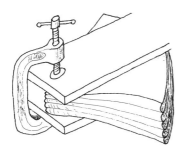

ESSENTIAL HAND SEWING STITCHES

Blanket stitch: This stitch is used to reinforce edges, traditionally in blankets. It is also very handy for attaching appliqué when you want to use a neat decorative stitch.

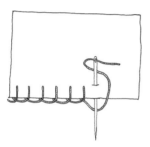

Going from left to right, insert the needle in position in the upper line and take a straight downward stitch, keeping the thread under the point of the needle. Pull up the stitch to form a loop, and repeat.

Blind stitch (also known as "slip stitch" or "invisible slip stitch"): If done properly, this stitch is almost invisible from both sides. It is often used for hemming, for appliqué, or to attach binding. Two versions are shown here—one is used if the needle does not go through all the layers of fabric, resulting in a stitch that will not be seen on the other side, and the other is used if the needle does go through to the other side but you do not want the stitch to be seen.

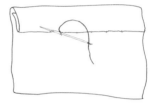

Working from right to left, take a stitch in the folded edge, then take a tiny stitch in the fabric directly opposite where the needle came out; continue by slanting the needle under the fold and coming up again vertically.

Running stitch: This simple stitch is used for quilting and creating decorative lines when one is embroidering. The basting stitch, used for keeping fabric in place while sewing, is similar but with very long stitches and spaces in between. The Sashiko stitch, a traditional Japanese decorative stitch, is another variation on the running stitch; it has a slightly longer stitch on the **Right** side of the fabric.

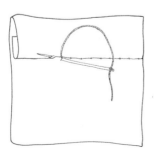

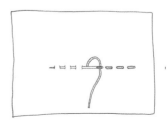

To create the running stitch, pass the needle in and out of the fabric, keeping both the stitch length and the space in between the same each time.

Whipstitch: This is a basic over-and-over stitch that is used for hemming or joining seams. Insert the needle into the fabric at an angle each time to make a neat, visible stitch.

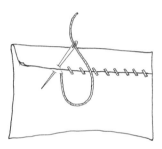

ESSENTIAL EMBROIDERY STITCHES

Backstitch: This stitch is very useful for drawing lines with thread.

To make a backstitch, take a backward stitch then bring the needle through in front of the first stitch.

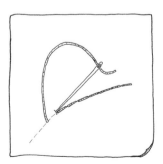

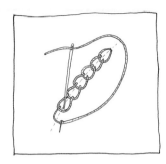

Chain stitch: Fundamental to embroidery, the chain stitch has many variations and is often used for flowers or to draw decorative lines.

Start by bringing the needle up from the back of the fabric at the beginning of your design line. Hold the thread against the fabric with your thumb, and insert the needle in the loop and bring it up a little farther down the line, creating a new loop. Insert the needle in the last loop made, while holding the thread down with the left thumb, and then bring it out a little lower than where it went in.

Cross-stitch: Probably the most widely used embroidery stitch, this stitch forms a cross shape that is versatile and simple to create.

You'll create two straight stitches, placed on the diagonal, with one crossed over the other. Many stitchers create rows of stitches in two steps, with the first half of the stitches worked in one direction and the crossover stitches made on the way back.

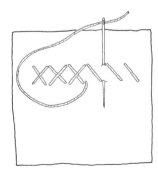

French knot: This simple knotting stitch is used for raised work, for filling in flowers, or for small details on faces.

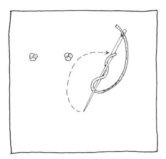

Insert the needle in the fabric from underneath and bring the thread out of the fabric and hold it down with your thumb; then twist it around the needle 3 or 4 times and insert the needle close to where the thread first came out. Pull the needle through to the back, leaving a small knot on the surface. It is very important to hold the thread with your thumb as long as possible so that the knot pulls nice and firm.

Satin stitch: This is a filler stitch in which lines are worked closely together so they touch across the width of the shape.

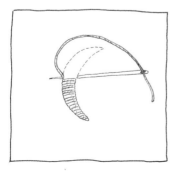

Take care to keep the edges even. You may want to outline your edges with a running stitch or back-stitch, and then take the satin stitches to the outside of this outline to create a neat edge.

Split stitch: Similar to the stem stitch, the needle splits the stitch as it emerges from the fabric. It is useful for drawing lines and shading in areas, and it looks a little like chain stitch. Use a thread that is soft and can easily be split by the needle.

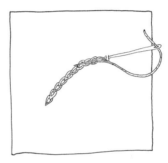

Work from left to right. Take small backstitches along your line and bring the needle up through the working thread.

Stem stitch: Here is another stitch that is very useful for drawing lines with thread.

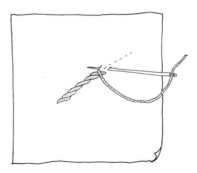

Stem stitch continued: Keep the needle pointed downward and work from left to right, keeping the thread below your needle and laying one stitch beyond the previous one in a continuous line.

Straight stitch: These single-spaced stitches lie flat on the surface and are made in any direction and any size. They are often used to create simple geometric lines or starbursts. The smaller version, called the "seed stitch," is used as a filling stitch.

Take the needle to the back at the end of the stitch and come up at the beginning of the next one.

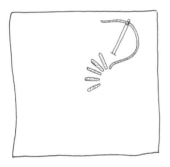

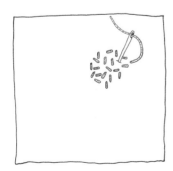

Traditionally, the three elements of the quilt—quilt top, batting, and backing—are placed on top of each other in a "quilt sandwich," with the quilt top and backing facing outward and the batting in the center. This is then basted together by machine or hand, and the binding is attached afterward.

The quilt top is the decorative pieced, appliquéd, or embroidered element; the batting is the soft inner layer that gives the quilt its warmth and thickness; and the backing is the practical element, which can be decorative or plain. The quilting holds the three layers together and can be hand sewn or machine stitched depending upon your desired outcome. The binding finishes the edges neatly.

BACKING

You can make a scrappy quilt back or use a whole piece of gorgeous fabric. It's a pity to put a whole lot of work into the quilt top only to use an inferior fabric on the back. It's best to use the same sort of fabric as the one you use on the front, in order to make washing and caring for the whole quilt simpler. So, if you are using cottons on the front, use cotton on the back and in the binding, too.

BATTING

Batting is the filler that gives loft and warmth to your quilt. There are heaps of different types of batting and all have different purposes and advantages. Use one that is appropriate for your project, taking into consideration what purpose the quilt will serve and how you plan to quilt it. If in doubt, ask for advice at your local quilting store. I am in the habit of using low-loft 100-percent cotton batting, because I find it easy to work with, store, wash, and quilt.

If you are planning on hand quilting, then you should use a low-loft (thin) batting. A high-loft batting is good for a winter quilt or a "tied" quilt, but it can be more difficult to work with.

Some experienced quilters say that wool batting is much easier for hand quilting, as the natural lanolin lubricates the needle. Synthetic batting doesn't shrink and can be machine washed, but it needs denser quilting to prevent the fibers from migrating to the surface (a phenomenon known as "bearding").

Alternative materials to use for batting include blanketing, flannel sheeting, or toweling. These can be good if the quilt is not going to be used as a bed covering. A mini quilt that will be used as a wall hanging may call for stiffening in the middle, such as in the Pensive Pansy Photo Quilt on page 48. If you are making a floor mat you might use toweling; for place mats, flannel sheeting might be the right thing. Most of the designs featured in this book use cotton batting as a standard, but a few do not use batting at all and instead make use of a heavy backing or layers of fabric.

BASTING

Before quilting, you will need to baste your quilt sandwich together. Basting temporarily holds the three layers of the quilt together while you are quilting. It is an important step to take, whether you are machine or hand stitching.

There are several ways of basting. Basting is usually done using long running stitches, known as "tacking stitches," over the whole quilt; however, you can also baste with safety pins placed at regular intervals. Generally, if you are hand quilting you will use tacking stitches, and if you are machine quilting you will baste with pins, but you might like to try basting spray or a heat-activated batting instead.

How to do it
Spread your quilt out on a tabletop or any flat surface large enough for your quilt.

Your backing cloth should be about 2 to 3 in/5 to 7.5 cm bigger than the quilt top on all sides. Place it right-side down, first smoothing it out with your hands or using a wide quilting ruler to ensure that it is wrinkle free. Stick the edges of the backing cloth down on your tabletop with masking tape to make sure it doesn't move—the tension should be even all across the backing cloth.

Lay your batting on top (it should be the same size as your backing) and smooth it down. Then place your quilt top, **Right** side facing up, over the batting and smooth it out. Center the quilt top evenly over the backing and batting.

SAFETY PIN BASTING

If you are basting with safety pins, place the pins in rows starting in the center and working your way out to each edge, pinning approximately every 6 in/15 cm.

STITCH BASTING

If you are stitch basting, first pin the quilt, placing pins every 6 in/15 cm over the quilt. Then use a bright contrasting thread and 1-in-/2.5-cm-long running (tacking) stitches. Starting in the middle, follow the lines of pins, working up and down until you come to the edge, and then start in the middle again and go out toward the other edge. Remove the pins.

SPRAY BASTING

With spray basting there is no need for pins and tacking stitches. This method is quick and effective and can be used for both hand and machine quilting. First, you will need to purchase high-quality fabric spray adhesive that will wash out. Ask at your local craft store for a recommendation if you are not sure which one to choose. When spraying, make sure to spray lightly; if you spray too heavily it can gum up your needles and your sewing machine will skip stitches. Protect your work surfaces in case you spray beyond the edges of your quilt, and be sure to spray in a well-ventilated room.

Lay your backing fabric facedown on a tabletop or floor that is protected by a plastic sheet, and tape it with masking tape so it's taut all around. Place your batting over the backing, making sure the edges match. Then, while it's still in place, roll your batting carefully onto a wide length of dowel (or use a broomstick with the bristles removed), and roll the batting to one end without lifting it, so that when you roll it back down it will still be correctly aligned.

Spray the adhesive along the edge of the backing closest to you, where you have rolled the batting, and place the end of the batting (still rolled on the dowel and still in the correct alignment) onto it. Then spray the next few inches of the backing, unroll the batting, and smooth. Continue to spray, unroll, and smooth your batting out incrementally until you have your whole piece of batting laid down over the backing. Smooth it out all over.

Then repeat the same steps with your quilt top. First place it over your batting, aligning it correctly and smoothing it carefully all over, then roll it up onto your dowel. It might be helpful to tape the far end of the fabric down; this will just help you roll it up without taking it out of alignment. Spray, unroll, and smooth, as you did earlier, in small increments. Then lift your quilt and turn it over, smoothing the backing down one last time. You are now ready to quilt.

Quilting

Quilting is the process of making small stitches all over the quilt and through all the layers. These stitches hold the three elements (quilt top, batting, and backing) together and make the whole quilt a sturdy, practical, and beautiful household item.

HAND QUILTING

Although it takes considerably longer, hand quilting has a special quality that cannot be duplicated by machine. I recommend hand quilting if you have hand pieced your quilt top, or if you want that singular look and feel that only hand quilting can give. Combining machine quilting with some hand-quilted elements, or adding decorative stitches such as Sashiko (see page 29) and embroidery, is also very effective. If you are not used to hand sewing, your hands will ache at first. But with the help of a quilting hoop, you can take your quilting with you to the couch or on holiday, and it can be a very relaxing pastime. If you are making a very large quilt, you might want to organize a quilting bee, a wonderful way to communicate and connect, which generations of women have embraced.

A number of quilts in this book are hand quilted. Imagine on page 156 uses free-form hand quilting, and the Road Transport Quilted Pillow (page 76) uses straight hand-quilted stitches. Other quilts have minimal hand quilting, such as Concentric Circles (page 114), which uses Sashiko stitches.

How to do it
You will need a spot with good light, a comfortable chair, a quilting hoop, and a thimble to ensure your hand-quilting experience is enjoyable. You will also need a quilting needle (these are called "betweens" and are smaller and stronger than normal needles). Experiment to see which length of needle feels right to you, and always use high-quality cotton thread in a coordinating color (you can purchase special quilting thread, which has a waxy coating, or run your regular cotton thread through beeswax to keep the thread from tangling). Have several needles threaded and ready to go, so that you won't have to stop and start once you get going. You will also need small clipping scissors and a seam ripper just in case.

Place the area that is to be quilted inside a quilting hoop (which is the same as an embroidery hoop), smoothing it on both sides. How taut you make the fabric is a personal choice; experiment with what feels right to you, and then tighten the screw on the hoop to hold it in place.

Start quilting by using a hidden quilter's knot, or a few backstitches hidden in a seam. Use a running stitch, pushing the needle down through all layers of the fabric (using your thimble-covered finger) until you feel it on your underneath finger.

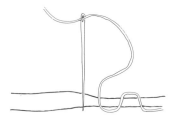

Rock the needle sideways and push it up to where you want it to come back through, and continue this step until you have a few stitches on the needle before pulling the thread through. How big you make the stitches is up to you; it's not the stitch size that matters, it's the consistency. Your hand-quilted stitches should be even and consistent on both sides of your quilt.

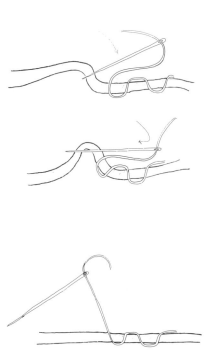

MACHINE QUILTING

Machine quilting is quick and utilitarian, but not as easy as you might think. It takes skill and patience to get the stitches even and prevent the fabric from puckering. Machine quilting is ideal for the mini quilts in this book.

There are two methods of machine quilting: stitching in straight lines and free-form quilting. For each method, the type of presser foot you use will make a big difference.

With machine quilting you can create various designs (see the quilting designs used in each project) just as you can with hand quilting, but you will need to use different presser feet depending on what you are doing. With grids or lines, "stitch in the ditch" (see page 38), and for outline quilting, try using a walking foot on your machine. The walking foot "walks" the top layer of fabric while the bottom layer moves along with the feed dogs.

Free-motion or freestyle quilting means quilting in a rambling design all over the quilt top without stopping. Your design can be a specific pattern or one you make up as you go along. If you want to free-motion quilt on your machine you will need to be able to lower the feed dogs. Using an embroidery foot or darning foot is also advisable. These are specifically made to be used with the feed dogs down, and they skim lightly across the fabric surface, preventing skipped stitches. With the feed dogs down, the speed with which you move the fabric controls the stitch length. Moving it at an even pace results in nice, even stitches, but this takes a lot of practice to master, so don't panic if your stitches are not uniform at first. Wearing rubber gloves or special quilting finger grips, although hot and uncomfortable, stops the fabric from slipping and helps you keep the path where you are sewing smooth.

STRAIGHT QUILTING

Grids or lines are usually used as background quilting, where you ignore the quilt top design and just quilt over the top of everything in an even pattern. When doing grids or evenly spaced lines you will need to stretch your quilt top on a table and tape it in place to prevent it from moving, and then use a set square to mark your grid design with tape or chalk pencil. You will then stitch in straight lines either by hand or by machine (using a walking foot) along your marked grid. You can attach a quilting guide bar to your machine to ensure that the grid lines are evenly spaced. The T-R-E-G-R-! Map Quilt on page 66 and Road Transport Quilted Pillow on page 76 both use a quilted grid design, while the Modern Geometric Quilt (page 124) is quilted with straight lines very close together.

With "stitch in the ditch" machine quilting, you stitch directly on top of the seam lines. This technique is often used if you want to hide the quilting. Keep the needle right on the seam line and use a walking foot if doing this by machine. Grasshopper in My Garden (page 90) and Power-line Sky (page 110) both use "stitch in the ditch" quilting before additional stitches are added.

In outline quilting, or echo quilting, you stitch ¼ in/6 mm out from the patchwork; it frames the pieces and enhances the design. If you are outlining unusual shapes you will need to lower the feed dogs and freestyle quilt by machine, or stitch by hand.

FREE-MOTION QUILTING

Whether you are quilting by hand or machine, you will find that freestyle quilting is a whimsical and fun alternative to structured quilting patterns. There are hundreds of designs to choose from. Leaf repeat patterns are used in the Blackbird at My Window quilt (page 86); or you can try an all-over random design (known as "stipple quilting") or an up-and-down squiggle design, as seen in the English Flower Garden Quilt (page 52). A Little Birdie Told Me (page 96) uses an all-over paisley flower design, while Follow Your Heart Art Quilt (page 56), uses a free-form text design.

TIPS FOR QUILTING BY MACHINE

When you are machine quilting, you will find it useful to have several filled bobbins at the ready, so you don't have to stop. When you do stop, make sure you keep the needle in place in the fabric to ensure there are no breaks in your design.

Do a tension check on a scrap of material before starting, and ensure that your bobbin tray is free from lint and you have enough thread on the bobbin.

Begin stitching in the center of the quilt and smooth out the area you will quilt first to prevent puckering. If you are doing a large quilt, you will need to roll it up to fit it under the machine arm.

The great thing about free-motion quilting is that you don't have to turn the fabric around; you just move in any direction you need.

BINDING

There are several ways to bind a quilt, and each of the methods has its place. When it's time to bind the quilt, you are nearly finished! A traditional mitered corner (see page 41) on your binding gives a very neat finish to your quilt. This type of binding is used for quite a few of the quilts in this book. Contrasting fabric can be used to create a frame, and coordinating fabric that blends into the quilt top can be used for a more subtle finish.

MAKING BINDING

Most of the project instructions in the book recommend making your own binding, which is incredibly easy to do. Of course, you can buy binding from your local fabric or craft store, and this is perfectly fine to use, but it comes in limited colors and widths. Making your own binding gives you unlimited design potential; you can make it any width using any fabric you choose, and you can make as much of it as you require. All you need are scissors or a rotary cutter, ruler, and mat to cut the fabric into lengths. You will also need an iron to crease it down the center.

Double fold or single fold

What's the difference between single- and double-fold binding? Double-fold binding is folded only once down the center of the strip and is sewn over the edge of the quilt with a double thickness of fabric for added protection. Single-fold binding is folded twice; each raw edge is folded toward the center of the strip and there is one thickness of fabric wrapping around the quilt edges.

Bias cut or straight cut

Bias binding is made from fabric cut on the bias (diagonal to the straight grain of the fabric). This gives the binding quite a bit more stretch, allowing it to be easily maneuvered around curves. Quilts usually have straight edges, so bias binding is often not necessary. However, it's useful when you are binding with piping, or binding curves.

To make continuous bias binding:

Cut a large square of fabric; the size will depend on how much binding you are making. A ½-yd/45-cm square will likely be enough for the projects in this book. Cut the square in half on the diagonal, making two triangles, and sew the triangles' outer sides together. Press the seam open.

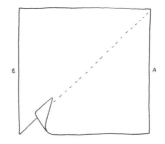

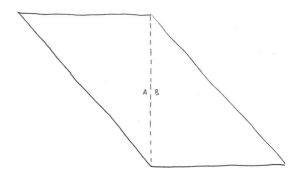

Use your ruler and a pencil to mark straight lines on the **Wrong** side of the fabric. Generally, you can make the strips 2 in/5 cm wide; if you are using a bias tape maker gadget, check the width it takes, because these come in different sizes.

Then sew the opposite edges of the now-sewn triangles, **Right** sides together, forming a cylinder shape. Offset one corner to match up with your line markings, and check to make sure that all the subsequent line markings also match up. Press the seam open.

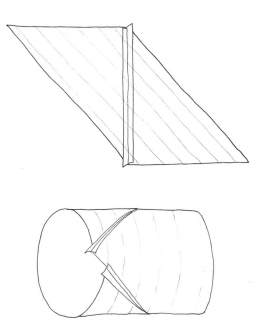

Start cutting with your scissors at the offset corner, and continue cutting along the line markings in one continuous line until you reach the end. You should end up with a long strip of fabric that is ready to turn into bias binding.

To make continuous straight-grain binding:

Take ⅛ yd/45 cm of fabric and mark 2-in-/5-cm-wide lines from selvage to selvage (or however wide you wish your binding to be). Then sew the selvage edges (see page 165) together, **Right** sides facing, leaving an offset of one line width (2 in/5 cm) and match up all the subsequent lines when you sew. Press the seam open. Then start to cut at the offset corner and continue cutting along the line until you reach the end. You will have a long strip of continuous straight-grain fabric ready to make into binding.

Whether you have made bias or straight-grain strips, the next step is the same to make single-fold binding. If you have a bias tape maker, feed one end into the gadget opening; as it comes out, the edges will be folded in toward the center. Make sure you have fed it in the right way first so that the **Right** side of the fabric is on the outside. Press it with a hot iron as you pull it out of the bias tape maker. Do the whole strip of fabric, and then press it down the center lengthwise to finish.

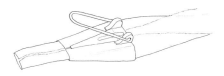

To make single-fold binding without a bias tape maker, first press the entire length of binding down the center lengthwise. Then fold in each raw edge to the center crease and press again along the entire length.

If making double-fold binding, just press the entire length once down the center, with **Right** sides facing out.

ATTACHING BINDING

Once you have made your binding and quilted your three layers together, you will want to attach the binding to your quilt.

If using double-fold binding, place the raw edges of the folded binding (without opening it up) on the quilt top and line up the raw edges of the quilt with the raw edges of the binding. If using single-fold binding, open up the binding and place it **Right**-side down on the quilt top, line up the raw edges of the quilt with one raw edge of the binding, and sew along the fold line.

Start sewing about 5 in/12.5 cm in from the start of the binding and stop just before you get to the end. Trim the binding ends so that you have a ½-in/12-mm seam allowance; open it up and join it together, at a 45-degree angle, and then place the raw edge back onto the quilt edge and finish sewing.

Alternatively, you could turn under the short, raw edge of binding, overlapping the starting point. This method is quicker but not nearly as neat.

the next section of binding up and away from you, perpendicular to the seam; then fold it neatly back down, aligned with the next side of the quilt edge to be sewn. You will end up with a loose triangle of excess fabric at the corner. Ignore this and don't sew it down, because you will use this excess fabric when folding the corner down on the opposite side.

Finally, turn the binding over to the back side of the quilt, enclosing the raw edge. At this point you can choose to hand sew with a blind stitch, or machine stitch, depending upon the style of the rest of your quilt.

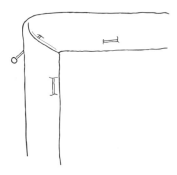

MITERED CORNERS

You can use the same method to get neat mitered corners, whether you are using single- or double-fold binding. As you sew up to a corner, stop and fold

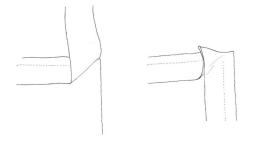

PILLOWCASE METHOD

One of the simplest ways to finish a quilt is not to bind it at all. Instead, use the pillowcase method (sometimes known as the "envelope method" or "bagging out") to sew the layers together before quilting. In this method, an opening is left on one edge and the layers are then turned **Right**-side out to create a neat finish. The quilting is done at the end. Quite a few of the quilts in this book are finished in this way, including the Circus Quilt on page 70, the Loopy Quilt (page 62), and Granny's Delight (page 132).

This is a really easy way to finish off your quilts; however, it isn't really suitable if you are planning on doing a lot of quilting, since you cannot quilt before using this finishing method.

Layer the quilt sandwich in a slightly different way than you would if you were quilting it first. Place the quilt top and quilt back **Right** sides together, and then place the batting on top.

Pin around the edges and sew ¼ in/6 mm in from the edge, leaving about a 5-in/12.5-cm opening in the middle of one side. Turn it **Right**-side out, just as if you were making a pillowcase cover. Use a chopstick or your fingers to push the corners out as much as you can, and press the edges all around. Close the opening with a neat blind stitch. And you are done.

ONE-STEP BINDING

One-step, single-fold binding is used in Two Heads Are Better than One and English Flower Garden Quilt on pages 146 and 52. This is a super-easy technique, but it's not so easy to get it absolutely neat. Take the single-fold binding and place it over the raw edge of the quilt so that it is evenly matched on both sides, and pin through all layers, mitering the corners. Then machine sew through all layers at once using either a straight stitch or a zigzag.

No hand sewing is required, but if you haven't matched up your binding correctly on both sides, then the stitching could be off. If it is, you will have to pick out the seams on some sections and sew over it again.

- -

FACING A QUILT

Another neat alternative for finishing a quilt is to face it. Facing is traditionally used around necklines in dressmaking to give a firm, invisible finish. Attaching a facing is similar to attaching binding; however, when folding it over to cover the edge, you take the whole of the binding toward the back, leaving the quilt at the front going right up to the edge (the facing is not seen from the front). This gives it a contemporary appearance but still allows you to quilt it in the usual way. The Modern Geometric Quilt on page 124 uses this method.

How to do it

Use your single-fold bias binding, made from the same material as your quilt back so it blends in nicely. Open up your binding and place the raw edge, **Right**-side down, onto the raw edge of the quilt top. Sew around, using the crease as a guide, and miter the corners as you come to them. If you can, press the edges open to ensure a really neat edge.

Then, instead of folding over the binding to enclose the raw edge of the quilt, you will fold the entire binding over to the back, so that the seam line is right on the edge of the quilt. Press. Pin into place and hand sew with a blind stitch to finish.

SELF-BINDING

A quick method for binding a quilt is to self-bind. With this method, you will need to first ensure that your backing fabric is quite a bit wider than the quilt top and batting on all sides, usually at least 2 in/5 cm per side. Then, once you have finished the quilting, you bring the backing fabric around to the front and sew as if it were binding. This is a good method for beginners or for a quick finish to your quilt. (See the Warbler Quilt on page 82.)

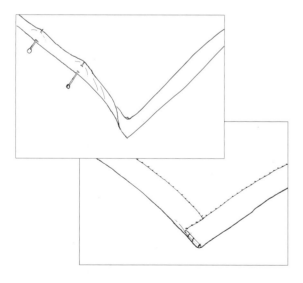

PRAIRIE POINTS

Prairie points are small squares of fabric folded into triangles and sewn onto the edging, slightly overlapping each other. They make for a very pretty decorative edging.

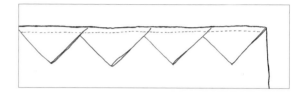

How to do it

Cut fabric squares; a 4½-in/11-cm square makes a 2-in-/5-cm-high folded triangle. Experiment with different sizes with squares of paper first. Fold the squares in half diagonally both ways and press.

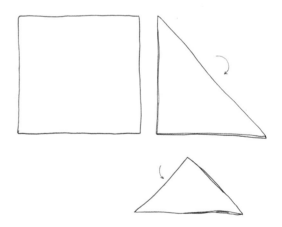

Attach these around the edge of the quilt either by sewing them in at the same time as using the pillowcase binding method, or by tucking them in around the edges after quilting (don't quilt right up to the edge if using this method). The Circus Quilt, on page 70, uses prairie points, or "bunting flags" along the top edge.

PIPING OR PIPED BINDING

One of the trickiest ways to bind a quilt is with a piped binding. Piping can add a very stylish twist and defined edge to your finished quilt or pillow. When using piping on a quilt you will need to either enclose it inside binding, as in the Power-line Sky (page 110) or put a backing onto it using the pillow-case method, as in the Road Transport Quilted Pillow (page 76).

You will need bias binding (see page 39) and cotton cord that is approximately ¼ in/6 mm in diameter.

Put your zipper foot onto your machine, and place the cord inside the binding, snug up against the fold. Stitch into place, with your zipper foot, sewing as close to the cord as you can get.

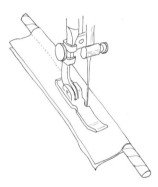

Attaching piping to your quilt or pillow
To attach your piping, you will need a zipper foot on your sewing machine. Place the raw edge of the piping against the raw edge of the quilt and pin into place. When you get to the corners, ease the piping around by clipping the seam allowance up close to the stitching line; this will allow the piping to curve around the corners.

To join the piping, weave in the ends of the cord, open up the ends of the binding fabric, and stitch together. Then finish sewing it down, or simply over-lap the two pieces of enclosed piping and fold to the back, stitching through in a straight line.

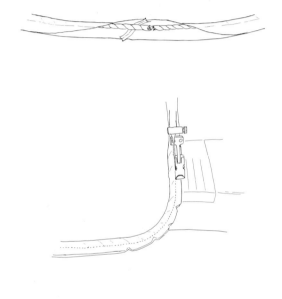

Whichever way you bind your quilt, make sure you choose a method that is going to suit the style of your quilt top and matches your available time and level of skill. Though none of the methods is particu-larly difficult, you'll need to make sure you have the time and energy to concentrate on getting it right if you are trying a method for the first time.

Displaying and Caring for Your Quilt

HANGING YOUR QUILT

Once you have finished making your quilt, you will want to display it.

CHECKLIST WHEN HANGING:

• Decide where you want to hang the quilt. Be sure the quilt is not in direct sunlight, since this will fade the fabrics.

• Avoid areas near heating vents, fireplaces, and walls that may heat up in the summer sun. Moisture is also bad for textiles, so be careful not to hang the quilt near evaporative coolers.

• Wherever you hang it, you should change your quilt's location every six months in order to protect it.

• When hanging your quilt you must distribute the weight evenly so you don't put any stress on the seams or the fabric.

• Never pierce the quilt with nails or use metal clips to hang it; this would damage the fabric.

To hang your quilt, attach a narrow sleeve to the back of the quilt and hang with a dowel or curtain rod. This distributes the weight evenly and will not damage the quilt. For a smaller quilt, you can use a picture hanger: just sew two buttonholes into either end of the hanging sleeve, insert a flat strip of wood into the hanging sleeve, and attach the two ends of a picture-hanging wire to the ends of the wooden strip. Hang as you would a painting.

MAKING A HANGING SLEEVE

Measure the width of your quilt and cut a strip of cotton or muslin fabric that is 8 in/20 cm wide and the same width as your quilt.

Hem the short edges by folding ¼ in/6 mm under and under again; then pin and sew. Fold the strip of fabric lengthwise, **Wrong** sides together, and sew along each of the long sides, making a tube. Lay it out so the seam lies in the center and press it open. You won't turn it **Right**-side out; instead, lay the open seam against the back of the quilt about ½ in/12 mm below where the binding finishes, and whipstitch, or blind stitch, the top and bottom edges of the sleeve to the quilt back, making sure not to stitch through to the quilt front.

An alternative method for short-term quilt hanging that doesn't involve sewing or attaching anything to the quilt is to securely attach a strip of stainless steel to the wall, just the width of the quilt. Then use tiny rare-earth magnets all along the front of the quilt, attaching it to the stainless-steel strip on the wall.

SIGNING AND LABELING QUILTS

It is important to label your quilt so others know who made it and when. Create a label, using a permanent marker, alphabet stamps and permanent ink, stencils, embroidery, or photo transfer fabric and then hand or machine appliqué the label onto the quilt backing. You can use fusible webbing to attach your label before sewing around the edges.

You can also directly sign your quilt in a corner somewhere on the front or back with permanent marker, either freehand, with a stencil, or with embroidery.

CARING FOR QUILTS

STORING

Store textiles in a dark, dry place such as an airing cupboard or linen cupboard. Store them either rolled up or folded, and unfold and refold your quilts twice a year to prevent permanent creases from forming. If you are storing quilts for long periods or the quilts contain delicate or antique fabrics, then wrap them in unbleached muslin or cotton before storing.

WASHING

Quilts containing delicate fabrics or unstable dyes should not be washed. If your quilt is hand pieced and quilted, then you will need to gently hand wash it with a mild detergent, rinse carefully, and lay it flat to dry. A machine-stitched quilt made with cotton can be washed in the washing machine on the gentle cycle.

Romantic

Romanticism is about the emotion of the "aesthetic experience," emphasizing intuition, imagination, and feeling. It began as an intellectual movement in Europe during the late eighteenth century, as a revolt against aristocratic lavishness and scientific rationalization. Today the Romantic style continues, characterized by its soft fabrics, florals, laces, and vintage linens. Crafting in the Romantic style is all about the emotions and senses evoked by various colors and textures. This style is very intuitive.

Alicia Paulson's Pensive Pansy Photo Quilt emphasizes floral fabrics in her simple squares design; Malka Dubrawsky's English Flower Garden Quilt uses English paper piecing to create a hexagon flower centerpiece; and Kajsa Wikman's sweet Follow Your Heart Art Quilt combines floral vintage fabrics, text, and simple appliqué.

IN THIS SECTION:

Pensive Pansy Photo Quilt 48 * *English Flower Garden Quilt* 52

Follow Your Heart Art Quilt 56 * Crazy Cats Quilt project offered online at www.chroniclebooks.com/miniquilts

This little quilt is easy to make up, and it gives you a chance to use a lot of beautiful bits from your scrap basket. Featuring your favorite photo, printed onto ink-jet-printer-ready photo fabric, this simple design relies on the patterns on the fabric to make it really special. Let your photo inform your fabric choices—in this quilt, the blues, purples, and greens of the pansies and the gardener's shirt inspired the delicate blossoms with a little linen thrown in for rustic effect.

Pensive Pansy Photo Quilt

by Alicia Paulson

Finished size: 14 in/35.5 cm square

Difficulty level:  **EASY**

MATERIALS

½ yd/46 cm total printed cottons and solid linen

Digital image 200 dpi (print quality), approximately 2 MB

1 sheet ink-jet-printer-ready white fabric

Cotton quilting thread

18-in/46-cm square heavyweight stabilizer for a stiff
    wall quilt or batting for a floppier quilt

18-in/46-cm square printed cotton for backing

Embroidery floss

1⅝ yd/1.5 m of ½-in/12-mm double-fold premade
    binding (you can purchase this at your local fabric store
    or make your own using the instructions on page 39)

EXTRA

Ink-jet printer/computer

TECHNIQUES

Binding: mitered corner binding

Decorative element: printing onto ink-jet-printer-ready fabric

Hand stitches: running stitch and slip stitch or blind stitch

NOTES

Seam allowances are all ¼ in/6 mm.

As you sew each section together, press the seams open before moving on to the next section.

When making the quilt sandwich, keep the stabilizer or batting and backing a bit larger than the quilt top in order to make it easier to line everything up evenly when stitching.

DIFFICULTY

This quilt is so simple to make. It involves easy sewing of squares; basic binding, minimal quilting, and some fun photo transfer designs.

CUTTING

1. Cut 7 pieces, 8½ x 2½ in/21.5 x 6 cm (6 printed cotton, 1 solid linen).

2. Cut 2 pieces, 6½ x 2½ in/16.5 x 6 cm (1 printed cotton and 1 solid linen).

3. Cut 9 squares, 2½ in/6 cm of assorted printed cottons.

MAKING THE PHOTO PATCH

1. Print the photo onto ink-jet printer-ready photo fabric, following the manufacturer's instructions for your particular fabric. Center the image, and cut the patch to 4½ x 6½ in/11 x 16.5 cm, leaving a ¼-in/6-mm white border around the entire photo.

ASSEMBLING THE QUILT TOP

1. Arrange your fabric pieces and photo patch like the diagram until you find a balance of color and tone that you like.

2. Sew the first strip of pieces together (column A) with the cotton thread. Stitch the pieces along their long edges, until you've created a column of seven pieces.

3. Stitch the two long pieces in column B along their long edges. Press and attach the short end of this pair to the top edge of the photo patch as in the diagram. Then stitch two of the small squares together and attach these to the bottom edge of the photo patch.

4. Then make column C by sewing seven of the small squares together in a row.

5. Now, attach the three columns together, with the photo column in the center. Press seams open to finish the quilt top, making it lie flat.

- -

FINISHING THE QUILT

1. Make a quilt sandwich, with the stabilizer piece centered on top of the backing piece and the quilt top placed **Right**-side up on top of the stabilizer. Pin around the edges and pin baste. Trim and square up the edges of the three layers.

2. Use six strands of embroidery floss to make heavy running stitches around the outside of the photo patch, on the seam line, creating a frame. Bury the tails of the floss in the back of the quilt at the starting and stopping points.

3. Bind the quilt, using the binding method described on page 41, ensuring you have neat mitered corners. Use a blind stitch to sew the binding at the back.

4. This is a hanging quilt, so attaching a hanging device is essential. You could use the method described on page 45 to attach a hanging sleeve; or you could sew a couple of loops onto each top corner with embroidery floss.

5. To sew loops, you will need to use two strands of embroidery floss. Make a knotless start on the back of the piece in an upper corner by making a couple of backstitches, securing the floss to the stabilizer and backing only (don't sew through to the front of the quilt). Make a ½-in/12-mm stitch, running the needle back under the stabilizer and backing only, and coming up where you started. Do one more stitch to fasten off and repeat for the opposite corner.

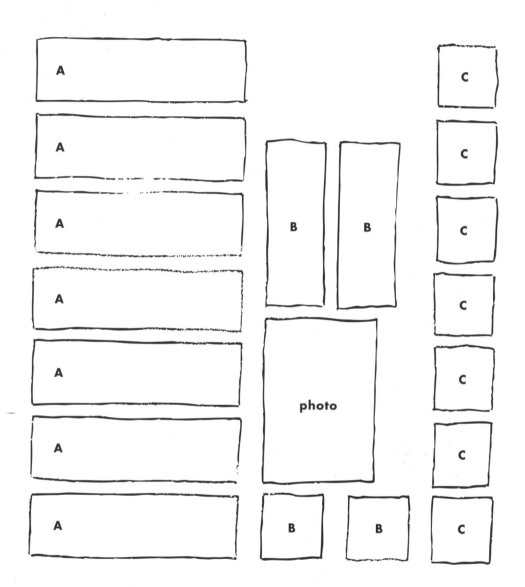

This quilt is a fusion of old and new, East and West, and uses a combination of techniques: embroidery, paper piecing, improvisational piecing, and quilting, with a mix of fabrics such as Japanese indigos, contemporary prints, and hand-dyed fabrics.

English Flower Garden Quilt

by Malka Dubrawsky

Finished size: 18 x 24 in/46 x 61 cm

Difficulty level: **MEDIUM**

MATERIALS

½ yd/46 cm total assorted cottons and linens in the same color family for quilt top

Cotton quilting thread

22 x 28 in/56 x 71 cm coordinating fabric for backing

22 x 28 in/56 x 71 cm 100 percent cotton batting

Embroidery floss (linen, wool, or cotton)

¼ yd/23 cm fabric for binding

EXTRAS

Brown paper or copy paper

Embroidery hoop

Supplies for basting

TEMPLATES

Hexagon template

TECHNIQUES

Piecing: English paper piecing and improvisational piecing

Quilting: free-motion machine quilting

Binding: one-step binding

Hand stitches: whipstitch, French knot, and blanket stitch

NOTES

Seam allowances are all ¼ in/6 mm.

The fabric is not prewashed; instead, it is washed after the quilt is assembled, in order to create a crinkly finish.

You can reuse the hexagon template and make one hexagon at a time, but if you want to work in assembly-line style you'll need to cut 19 hexagon templates out of paper and you are ready to go.

The background uses improvisational piecing. Use the guidelines on page 22 to create your own unique background; however, if you want to re-create the quilt shown here, use the diagram provided.

DIFFICULTY

Although this quilt is not difficult, it does take some time and care. It involves a bit of hand stitching and freestyle quilting and requires you to wrangle with the English paper piecing method, but once you get the hang of it you will be whipping these up in no time.

CUTTING

1. Cut strips of fabric in various widths to surround your central flower block and to create your improvised quilt background. You will need approximately 9 thin strips that immediately surround the flower block and 5 wide strips for the outer border.

2. Cut one 7-x-7½-in/17-x-19-cm piece of fabric for the center panel.

3. Cut 1½-in/4-cm strips, on the straight grain, out of the binding fabric.

4. Copy the hexagon template onto brown or copy paper and cut it out.

5. Select the fabric for your flower. There are three rings of hexagons and each ring is made out of a different fabric. When cutting, leave ¼ in/6 mm extra fabric all around. Pin the hexagon templates to your fabric: cut 1 hexagon for the center of the flower, 6 hexagons for the second ring of petals in the flower, and 12 hexagons for the third ring of petals in the flower. Each sewn hexagon should measure approximately 1½ in/4 cm diagonally from point to point.

MAKING THE FLOWER

1. Use the English paper piecing method on page 21 to make up your 19 hexagons with your fabric and templates, press, and prepare the hexagons so they are ready to assemble.

2. Hand sew the hexagons together using a whip-stitch with cotton thread. Start with the center of the flower hexagon, and attach the second ring of hexagon pieces one at a time. Then follow with the third ring of hexagon pieces, thus creating your hexagon flower. Remove the paper templates and press.

3. Pin the flower to your center panel background fabric and place in an embroidery hoop. Embroider French knots densely in the center flower hexagon.

4. Readjust the embroidery hoop so that you can stitch down the edges of the flower. Use a blanket stitch with a coordinating thread to simultaneously embroider and appliqué the flower to its back-ground fabric.

ASSEMBLING THE QUILT TOP

Start with the center flower panel, and attach one of your thin fabric strips to one side of it, and turn to add another thin strip to another side. Continue turning and sewing the remainder of your thin strips around the center panel and end with the widest strips, following the general guidelines for a log cabin block on page 21. Press all seams to one side, and press the whole quilt top.

FINISHING THE QUILT

1. Make a quilt sandwich, with backing fabric, batting, and quilt top. Baste in position using your preferred basting method—tacking stitches, safety pins, or basting spray.

2. Machine quilt the entire quilt using a dense free-style squiggle pattern and cotton quilting thread.

3. Make your binding using the continuous bind-ing technique (on page 39) and attach to your quilt,

using your preferred method. The binding on this quilt has been attached using the one-step method, with mitered corners, and a zigzag stitch.

4. Machine wash and machine dry the quilt to enhance its texture.

5. To hang the quilt, attach a hanging sleeve to the back, following the instructions on page 45.

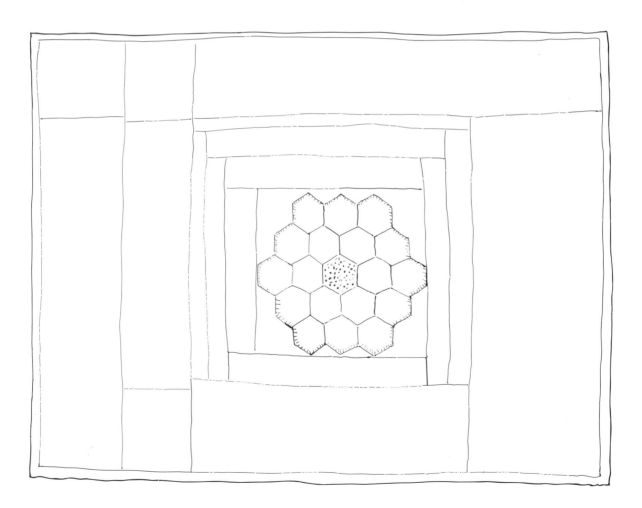

This adorable mini quilt is made with a much-loved and now-faded piece of floral linen. This quilt may be small, but its message reminds us to stop and think about what we want most from our lives. Feel free to improvise your own text quilted message.

Follow Your Heart Art Quilt

by Kajsa Wikman

Finished size: 10 x 11½ in/25 x 29 cm

Difficulty level: **MEDIUM**

MATERIALS

2 small scraps deep pink or red for the log cabin centerpiece and the heart template

Scraps of cotton fabrics in four different pastels to make binding and log cabin block

½ yd/46 cm linen or cotton fabric in off-white with faded flowers

1 small scrap blue (or coordinating fabric of your choice) for bird template

14 x 15½ in/35.5 x 39 cm cotton fabric in a pastel color for backing

14-x-15½-in/35.5-x-39-cm 100 percent cotton batting

Machine embroidery thread

Cotton quilting thread

Embroidery floss

EXTRAS

Rotary cutter, ruler, and cutting mat

Paper-backed adhesive

Quilt basting spray

Chalk pencil

Embroidery or darning foot for free-motion stitching

TEMPLATES

Bird appliqué

Heart appliqué

List continues next page

NOTES

Seam allowances are all ¼ in/6 mm.

If the free-motion quilted text seems challenging, you can use a chalk pencil to prewrite the text on your quilt top. Your own handwriting will make it unique! Kajsa quilted a little heart when there was not enough space for a whole word.

To re-create the romantic retro feel of this small quilt, you will need to use linen, vintage if you can find it, or an off-white cotton with a soft floral design.

DIFFICULTY

This is such a small quilt that it won't take you long at all to whip it up; the most challenging part is the free-motion text quilting. Practice the free-motion quilting on a scrap of fabric first, if you like. Have fun with it.

CUTTING

1. Cut one 1½-in/4-cm square out of the deep pink or red fabric scrap for the log cabin block centerpiece.

2. Cut one 15-x-1-in/38-x-2.5-cm strip from each of the four pastel fabrics.

3. Cut one 18-x-1-in/46-x-2.5-cm strip from the off-white fabric.

4. Cut one 5½-in/14-cm square from the off-white fabric.

5. Cut one 7-x-10½-in/17-x-26.5-cm piece from the off-white fabric.

6. Cut 1-in-/2.5-cm-wide strips from the off-white fabric (the same fabric you are using for the main background of the quilt) (on the straight grain) and randomly join in four small pieces of the pastel fabrics for a hint of color; use this to make binding using the instructions on page 39. You will want to cut enough off-white strips so the total length of the pieced binding will easily go around the perimeter of your quilt.

ASSEMBLING THE QUILT TOP

1. You will start by making the log cabin block. Take the pink or red center square and sew strips of the off-white fabric to two adjoining sides; then take a pastel fabric strip and join to the two opposite sides. Continue by alternating between the off-white fabric strip and a different pastel fabric strip each time. Sew, press, and cut after joining each strip. (See the instructions for log cabin quilts on page 21.) The finished block should be a 5½-in/14-cm square; trim to size if needed.

Continued from page 57

TECHNIQUES

Piecing: log cabin block

Appliqué: machine raw-edge appliqué

Binding: mitered corner binding

Quilting: free-motion machine quilting

2. Sew the off-white side of the log cabin square to the 5½-in/14-cm off-white fabric square. Press seam open and then press to one side.

3. Join the log cabin section with the 7-x-10½-in/ 17-x-26.5-cm piece and press seams to one side.

APPLIQUÉING

1. Trace the appliqué templates onto paper and flip over to create reverse copies onto paper-backed adhesive. Cut out the pieces from the adhesive paper. Iron these pieces onto the **Wrong** side of the fabric you are using for your appliqué pieces, and cut out.

2. Place the bird and heart appliqué pieces adhesive-side down onto the quilt top and press with a hot iron to bond them to the quilt top. With the embroidery thread, machine sew carefully, using a short straight stitch around the edges. With your machine appliqué or embroidery foot, sew a beak and feet onto the bird using a straight stitch.

FINISHING THE QUILT

1. Make a quilt sandwich, with backing fabric, batting, and quilt top. Hand or spray baste all the layers together. Adjust your sewing machine for free-motion quilting, drop the feed dogs on your machine, and use a free-motion embroidery foot. Use a chalk pencil to mark the text before you quilt, if needed. Quilt your text design, starting from the upper left corner of the quilt. Make a few stitches in place to secure the cotton quilting thread at the start and finish of your quilting.

Follow
your heart.
heartees

2. With the chalk pencil, draw the flying track for the bird freehand, and then stitch by hand with embroidery floss in a contrasting color using a simple running stitch.

3. With the pieced binding strip, press to make single-fold binding (see instructions on page 39). Bind the quilt, following the instructions on page 41 for traditional binding with mitered corners.

4. To hang the quilt, attach a hanging sleeve to the back, following the instructions on page 45.

Playful

The quilts in this section are playful and interactive—they are made to light up the imagination and inspire learning. They make use of materials and design in a creative way, often utilizing texture and color to help tell a story or create a feeling.

Betz White's Loopy Quilt, a squiggly felt mat, is a delight of texture and color; Lizette Greco's T-R-E-G-R-! Map Quilt rolls up into a scroll for imaginative play; Alix McAlister's Circus Quilt has a secret pocket with a hidden toy; while the Road Transport Quilted Pillow by Kristine Lempriere uses whimsical appliqué.

IN THIS SECTION:

Loopy Quilt 62 * T-R-E-G-R-! Map Quilt 66

Circus Quilt 70 * Road Transport Quilted Pillow 76

This playful mini quilt combines the rich color
and texture of wool felt with the earthy beauty
of natural unbleached linen. It is a simple
design—a sort of freestyle reverse appliqué,
where the felt is sewn and then cut away to
reveal a subtle background.

Loopy Quilt

by Betz White

Finished size: 12½ x 16½ in / 32 x 42 cm

Difficulty level: **EASY**

MATERIALS

4 x 12 in/10 x 30.5 cm wool felt in 4 different colors

12½ x 16½ in/32 x 42 cm unbleached linen, for quilt top

12½ x 16½ in/32 x 42 cm printed cotton, for backing

12½ x 16½ in/32 x 42 cm cotton low-loft batting

Cotton thread

14 multicolored felt balls, each ½ in/12 mm

EXTRAS

Tailor's chalk or disappearing fabric marker

Small embroidery scissors

Embroidery or darning foot for free-motion stitching

Fray-check spray

Hand-sewing needle

TECHNIQUES

Appliqué: free-motion machine stitching

Binding: pillowcase method

NOTES

Seam allowances are all ¼ in/6 mm.

Prewash all fabrics, including wool felt, separately. Press out the wrinkles.

For zigzag stitch, use a stitch width of number 5 and a length of number 2.5, with matching thread.

DIFFICULTY

This is such a fun and quick little quilt to make up—there is only minimal hand sewing. You will need to lower the feed dogs on your machine and do some free-motion stitching—if you haven't tried this before, do a little practice run first.

CUTTING

Cut one 4-x-12-in/10-x-30.5-cm rectangle of felt in each of the four different colors.

ASSEMBLING THE QUILT TOP

1. Align the four rectangles of felt side by side, with the 12-in/30-cm sides touching. Zigzag the rectangles together, two at a time, by butting the raw edges together and straddling both pieces with a wide zigzag stitch. Repeat until all four rectangles are joined together. Press flat.

2. Place the now-joined large rectangle of felt on top of the linen quilt-top piece and pin to secure them together.

3. Now comes the fun part: draw a random "squiggle" design, with tailor's chalk or disappearing fabric marker, onto your pieced felt rectangle.

4. Lower the feed dogs on your machine (see page 15 for more about this), and use a free-motion presser foot to enable you to sew freely over your squiggle pattern. Follow your squiggle design to sew along the lines you have drawn, and stitch the felt to the linen. Be sure to remove the pins as you approach them. Stop periodically and check your design to see that it looks balanced and adjust if you need to.

5. Use small embroidery scissors to carefully cut away the felt, trimming about ⅛ in/3 mm from either side of the stitch lines. Take care not to cut into the linen background. Continue trimming and removing the felt to reveal your design! When you are finished, put a drop of fray-check spray on the spots where the felt is zigzagged together.

FINISHING THE QUILT

1. Assemble the quilt top, batting, and backing, using the pillowcase method, as shown on page 41. Place the quilt top and quilt back **Right** sides together. Center the batting on the **Wrong** side of the quilt top. Stitch ¼ in/6 mm in from the edge, leaving a 6-in/15-cm opening on one edge. Trim the seam allowances at the corners and turn **Right**-side out. Tuck the raw edges of the gap under and pin, and then topstitch around the entire quilt ⅛ in/3 mm from the edge. Press.

2. Lay out your felt balls along the short edges in your desired configuration. Double thread a hand-sewing needle, and attach each by stitching through the center of the ball and then taking a stitch through all layers at the edge of the quilt. Bind off. Repeat until all of the balls are attached.

3. This cute and colorful quilt can be used as a home accent for a tabletop or displayed on a wall.

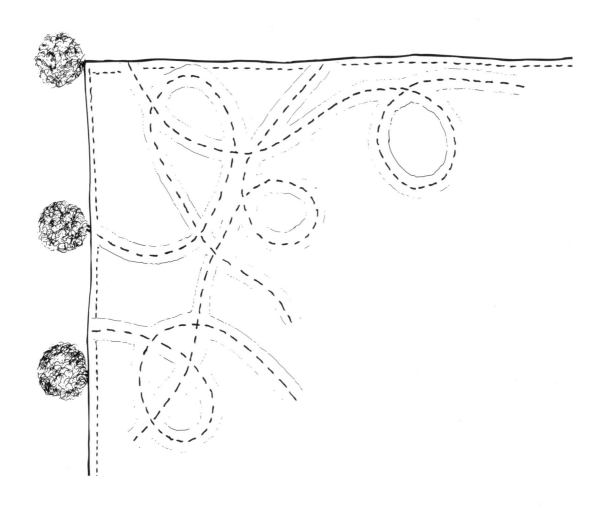

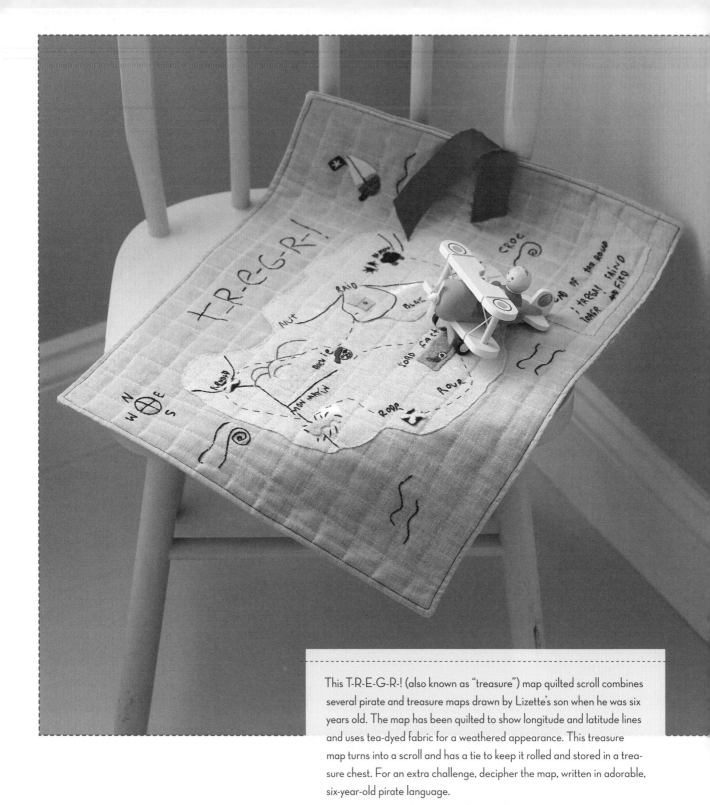

This T-R-E-G-R-! (also known as "treasure") map quilted scroll combines several pirate and treasure maps drawn by Lizette's son when he was six years old. The map has been quilted to show longitude and latitude lines and uses tea-dyed fabric for a weathered appearance. This treasure map turns into a scroll and has a tie to keep it rolled and stored in a treasure chest. For an extra challenge, decipher the map, written in adorable, six-year-old pirate language.

I-R-E-G-R-! Map Quilt

by Lizette Greco

Finished size: 13 x 17 in /33 x 43 cm

Difficulty level: **MEDIUM**

MATERIALS

12-in/30-cm square beige fabric for island and legend

14-x-18-in/35.5-x-46-cm piece light-blue fabric for ocean background

14-x-18-in/35.5-x-46-cm piece cotton batting

14-x-18-in/35.5-x-46-cm piece beige fabric for backing

Embroidery floss in black, white, green, light blue, yellow, and gray

Bits of wool felt in white, brown, red, yellow, and off-white for appliquéd details

Cotton quilting thread in white and black

17-x-1-in/43-x-2.5-cm strip red fabric for tie

EXTRAS

Strong black tea

Thin iron-on interfacing, in case you need to add some weight to any of your recycled fabrics and keep them from fraying (optional)

Fray-check spray

Iron-on transfer pencil, carbon paper, or tissue paper

Tailor's chalk, or disappearing-ink fabric pen

14-x-18-in/35-x-45-cm piece of cardboard, for stretching and pinning quilt

Quilting ruler

TEMPLATES

Embroidery elements

Whole quilt map

NOTES

Seam allowances are all ¼ in/6 mm.

This quilt uses all recycled fabrics, but feel free to improvise and use whatever you have on hand.

This design uses the tear-away method to transfer the embroidery design. Alternatively, you could use an iron-on pencil or carbon paper to transfer the design.

DIFFICULTY

Although this quilt has quite a few fiddly details, it is fun to make, keeping you interested at each step along the way.

CUTTING

Using the templates provided, trace and cut your pieces.

PREPARING THE ISLAND PIECES

1. Tea dye the fabric that will be used for the island and legend. Dye the fabric before cutting in case of shrinkage. Please refer to the directions on page 26.

2. Cut 1 tea-dyed (or beige fabric) island and legend (draw the island freehand or copy the template provided).

3. Apply iron-on interfacing to add some stiffness to the island and legend pieces, apply fray-check spray around edges, and allow pieces to dry.

List continues next page

ASSEMBLING THE QUILT TOP

1. To transfer the embroidery details onto the quilt top, you can use an iron-on transfer pencil or carbon paper, or you might like to draw your own design freehand. Or you can instead trace the details onto tissue paper and sew through this onto your fabric; the paper will then be torn away when the sewing is finished. Once you have traced the island details, text, and images onto several pieces of fine tissue paper, cut and pin the papers into position onto the island.

2. Embroider the text onto the fabric, using a stem stitch (embroider through the paper if using; gently tear the paper away once you have completed each detail). Then embroider the map lines onto the map, using both running stitch and chain stitch to differentiate the different paths.

3. Trace and cut the felt for the appliqué details using the templates provided. Blind stitch them in place with the same color thread and embroider the additional details using stem stitch or chain stitch. Press.

Continued from page 67

TECHNIQUES

Decorative element: tea dyeing

Hand stitches: stem stitch, running stitch, chain stitch, and blind stitch

Appliqué: raw edge appliqué

Binding: pillowcase method

Quilting: Straight line machine quilting

4. After you have completed the embroidered and appliquéd details on the island, pin and stitch it onto your ocean (blind stitch in place then use a running stitch around the edge to frame it). This becomes the top of your mini quilt.

5. Transfer the embroidered details for the ocean onto the ocean fabric and embroider and appliqué the pirate ship, waves, and directions (N, S, E, and W).

6. Create the legend by using the embroidery method as before, and then sew, with a blind stitch, onto the bottom corner of the map.

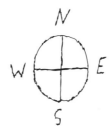

FINISHING THE QUILT

1. Once you are done with your quilt top, press your three layers (top, batting, and back of quilt) and use the pillowcase method to finish the edges of the quilt (see instructions on page 41). Loosely hand stitch the opening closed (you will remove this later when you topstitch with your sewing machine).

2. Stretch the quilt onto a piece of cardboard by pinning the edges all around, or tape it down onto a table, in order to keep the quilt straight while you draw the grid lines across and down the quilt (use tailor's chalk or a disappearing-ink fabric pen for this). Make perpendicular marks along the top, bottom, and sides of the quilt, using your quilting ruler, 1 in/2.5 cm apart, and then use your ruler to connect the lines.

3. Remove the quilt from the cardboard and baste the layers together using safety pins every row. Use white thread to machine stitch the lines, first down and then across, always beginning to sew from the center of your quilt toward the outside.

4. When you have finished the quilting, remove the loose stitching from the quilt opening and machine stitch around the quilt, ⅛ in/3 mm from the edge, with black thread, to frame and close the opening.

5. Apply fray-check spray to the length of red fabric and let dry. Roll the mini quilt map into a scroll and tie the red ribbon around it. Stitch the ribbon in place on the back with a few hand stitches, so it won't fall off and get lost.

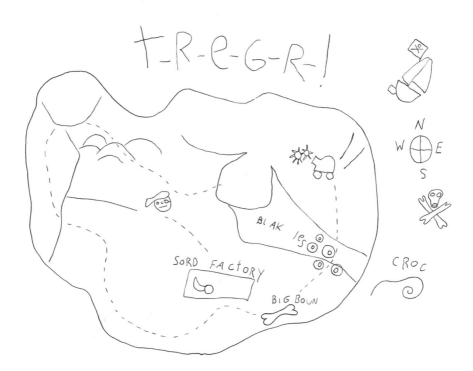

The circus conjures up images of exotic textiles and luscious fabrics; it is a place of imagination, secrets, and magic. This circus quilt, with its tent-door secret pocket, hides a toy circus horse and is finished with a colorful bunting top.

Circus Quilt

by Alix McAlister

Finished size: 20 x 25 in/50 x 63.5 cm

Difficulty level: **TRICKY**

MATERIALS

15 x 18 in/38 x 46 cm red fabric

16 x 22 in/40.5 x 56 cm white fabric

14 x 26 in/35.5 x 66 cm blue fabric (faded denim)

8 x 10 in/20 x 25 cm fabric for the horse

Small scraps ¼- to ⅜-in-/6-mm- to 1-cm-wide ribbon for the horse

Small scraps colorful fabric for bunting and tent door

Thread in coordinating colors for hand and machine sewing

White cotton thread

Off-white embroidery floss

22 x 26 in/56 x 66 cm muslin (or other plain cotton) for lining

22 x 26 in/56 x 66 cm printed cotton for backing

Dark blue thread

Toy stuffing

Embroidery floss

EXTRAS

Tape

Fabric pen

Rotary cutter, ruler, and cutting mat

List continues next page

NOTES

Seam allowances are all ¼ in/6 mm, unless otherwise indicated.

This quilt uses recycled fabrics; you may use fabrics from your scrap bag, cut-up old clothes, or new fabrics, but they must be sturdy, child friendly, and washable, because this is a playful quilt.

This quilt is like a jigsaw puzzle with 24 unique pieces. It depends on all the different pieces fitting together, so accurate cutting and numbering are important. Number each piece on the back as you cut.

The quilt will be made in two main sections; first the tent sides, and second the tent roof, with a rectangle of sky attached.

DIFFICULTY

This quilt is not an improvisational, carefree kind of quilt. It requires careful cutting, labeling, and sewing.

CUTTING

1. First trace or photocopy the pattern pieces and cut them out. Lay all the pattern pieces for the same color on their fabric (red, white, and blue), and hold them in place with tape rolled up underneath. Or you might like to cut the pattern pieces out of freezer paper, which can be held in place temporarily on the fabric while you are cutting, if you first press with a hot iron.

2. Use a fabric pen to trace around the pattern pieces and write their corresponding number in the seam allowance.

3. Use a fabric pen to mark the registration points to help with lining up the pieces on each corner of the pattern.

4. Remove the paper pattern pieces and put aside, and then cut out the fabric (if you used freezer paper you can leave the paper pattern pieces in place until you are ready to sew). Make sure you draw and cut out the pieces as carefully and accurately as possible.

5. Cut out 2 pieces each of the horse body and tail, using the horse template. Cut 4 pieces of ribbon, 1¾ in/ 4.5 cm long, for the horse's mane and 1 (4½-in-/ 11-cm-long) piece of ribbon to go around the body.

6. Cut 1 rectangle (20½-x-5 in/52-x-12.5 cm) of the blue fabric, which forms the top piece of the quilt.

7. Cut 1 square, 8½ in/21.5 cm, of any fabric for the pocket lining. This will not be seen.

8. Cut 9 squares, 3 in/7.5 cm, from a variety of colorful fabric for the bunting.

9. Cut strips of various sizes; all must be at least 8½ in/21.5 cm wide for the tent door section.

Continued from page 71

TEMPLATE AND PATTERN PIECES

Pattern pieces for circus quilt

Horse template

TECHNIQUES

Binding: prairie points and pillowcase method

Hand stitches: running stitch, satin stitch, and whipstitch

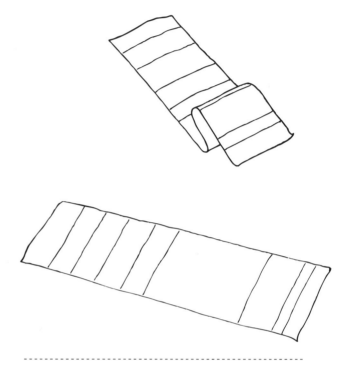

ASSEMBLING THE TENT SIDES

1. Start with the colorful striped tent door section; this section holds the secret pocket. Choose colorful strips of fabric for the top and bottom parts of the door. Sew these scraps together into a strip crosswise and press the seams open; then use the pattern templates to cut out the two sections for the door from these sewn strips of fabric.

2. Attach the 8½-in-/21.5-cm-square pocket lining piece between the two door sections, with **Right** sides together. Press the seams of your now-long strip of fabric open, and fold the pocket lining section so that the seams of the scrappy door sections meet. Press and trim any excess fabric and pin the pocket closed. Sew this section in where the door is marked in the illustration.

3. Line up the entire set of pattern pieces for the tent side on a flat surface. Baste the pieces together in pairs. (This basting step is important for accuracy; it will allow you to achieve the subtle curves in the design.)

4. Machine stitch the pairs of basted pieces. Now, line up the machine-stitched pairs and baste those together. Then machine stitch until you have all the pieces of the bottom section of the tent sewn together. Remove the basting stitches and press the seams toward the dark-colored fabric.

ASSEMBLING THE TENT ROOF

1. *See illustration page 75* Repeat the previous steps to sew the roof section pieces of the tent together, first basting and then sewing in pairs, and being careful to note the registration points. Take particular care where the pieces meet at the roof peak. Press the pairs flat, seams open, before you continue basting the next pairs together, since you may catch other roof segments while sewing near the roof peak. Pin other pieces out of the way to ensure that this doesn't happen.

2. Toward the peak there may be a little bunching; you will need to carefully cut away any excess seam allowance or bulk and press seams open, or as flat as you can.

3. Next, add the pieces of sky that border the tent roof, again basting first. Then attach the rectangle of sky across the tent roof section.

JOINING THE TENT SIDES AND ROOF

1. Sew the tent roof and the tent side sections together. Baste together following the curve where

they meet, and remember that the alternating red and white pieces of the roof and sides should meet up at the ¼-in/6-mm seam allowance. Don't worry if it isn't perfect; more important is that the tent door and roof are lined up. Press flat.

2. Due to the many curved seams and various types of fabric used, you may need to trim and square up the edges. Use a rotary cutter, ruler, and cutting mat, or draw straight lines with a ruler and fabric pen and trim with scissors.

MAKING THE BUNTING FLAGS (PRAIRIE POINTS)

1. Follow the instructions on page 43 for making prairie points, using the 9 squares you cut for this project. After making your bunting flags (prairie points), choose the order you want for the flags and place them with the triangles pointing downward

along the top edge of the quilt (the wide edges of the triangles and top raw edge of the quilt will be aligned).

2. Place the first and last flag ¼ in/6 mm from the edge of the quilt top, making sure each one overlaps the next slightly in the same direction. Start with the left-hand corner flag. This will ensure that when you sew it with the machine you will be sewing with the overlap, and not against it.

3. Pin the flags into position and then machine baste in place, using a longer stitch length and looser tension than usual, with a ⅛-in/3-mm seam allowance. You will attach the backing using the pillowcase method, and the bunting flags will then be in the correct position to be sewn into place at the same time as the backing.

- -

FINISHING THE QUILT

1. Embroider the moon on the top left rectangle of sky with white cotton thread, using a running stitch to outline the silhouette of a crescent moon. Then, using all 6 strands of off-white embroidery floss, fill in the moon using satin stitch.

2. Make a quilt sandwich by placing the muslin lining on the bottom, then the backing fabric **Right**-side up, and the quilt top **Right** sides facing in. Smooth flat and pin all around the edges.

3. Machine sew all around the quilt, leaving a 5-in / 12.5-cm opening through which you can turn the entire quilt **Right**-side out. Leave this gap along the side of a segment of the sky, not along the top edge bunting.

4. Trim all the excess lining and backing fabric. Snip the corners and turn the quilt **Right**-side out. Poke the corners from the inside with a chopstick and iron flat. Then topstitch the sky section of the quilt with dark blue thread (you can leave the bobbin white underneath) about ⅛ in/3mm from the edge; this will also close the opening that you left for turning the quilt **Right**-side out. Topstitch the tent part of the quilt with white thread.

- -

MAKING THE TOY HORSE

1. Sew the 2 horse tail pieces **Right** sides together with a ⅛ in/3 mm seam allowance, leaving the short end open to turn. Turn the tail **Right**-side out and topstitch as you like. Lay one piece of the horse body faceup, place tail so that the short end lines up with the rear-end raw edge, and pin (the tail should be lying flat inside the body). Fold the 1¾-in/4.5-cm ribbon pieces in half, and place where the mane would be, matching up the ribbon raw edges with the horse body raw edges. Baste the tail and mane in place.

2. Take the other horse body piece and place it facedown on top of the first piece; pin together and stitch all the way around with a ⅛-in/3-mm seam allowance, leaving an opening at the belly to turn the body **Right**-side out. Clip the seam allowance along any curves and corners. Use a chopstick to push out the legs, ear, and nose. Stuff the body with toy stuffing, and whipstitch the opening closed. Attach the 4½-in/11-cm piece of ribbon around the body and hand sew in place.

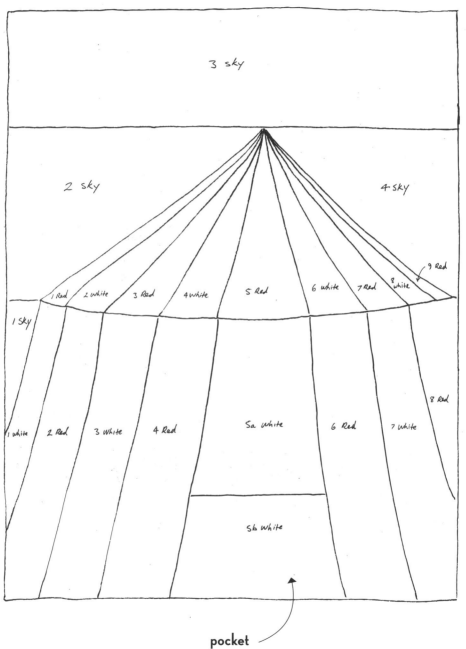

3 sky

2 sky

4 sky

1 Red · 2 white · 3 Red · 4 white · 5 Red · 6 white · 7 Red · 8 white · 9 Red

1 sky

1 white · 2 Red · 3 White · 4 Red · 5a White · 6 Red · 7 White · 8 Red

5b White

pocket
colorful pocket section goes here

This mini quilt has been made into a soft, practical cushion cover—perfect for little boys and also ideal as a special reading pillow. If you like the design but don't need another pillow, you can follow the instructions until the piping stage, at which point you can bind it and use it as a wall quilt.

Road Transport Quilted Pillow

by Kristine Lempriere

Finished size: 24 x 25 in/60 x 63 cm

Difficulty level:  **TRICKY**

List continues next page

MATERIALS

- 24-in/60-cm length paper-backed iron-on adhesive
- Small pieces contrasting fabric in a neutral shade for details on the cars (wheels, bumpers, and exhaust pipes)
- Small pieces colored fabric with small prints for the cars and trucks
- 31-in/80-cm square solid cotton for quilt front
- Thread in coordinating colors to match appliqué fabrics
- 31-in/80-cm square solid cotton for backing (if you are making this as a cushion, this fabric will end up inside so you can use any fabric you like)
- 28-in/71-cm square light cotton, machine-washable quilt batting
- 20-in/50-cm square printed fabric to make 4 yd/3.6 m of 2-in/5-cm-wide bias strips for piping
- 4 yd/3.6 m (¼-in-/6-mm-diameter) cotton cord for piping
- 31-in/80-cm square contrasting fabric for cushion back
- 24-in/60-cm square pillow form
- 3 medium-size buttons in a color that coordinates with piping fabric
- Quilting thread in same color as quilt front for hand quilting

EXTRAS

- Water-soluble fabric pen
- Quilt basting spray
- Permanent fabric pen

NOTES:

Seam allowances are all ¼ in/6 mm.

The quilt was machine appliquéd using a decorative blanket stitch. If your machine does not have this stitch, try a zigzag stitch; change the zigzag's length and width to get the desired effect. If you want stronger outlines for your shapes, use a wider and shorter zigzag.

The machine appliqué in this quilt is quite detailed, but it's really a case of following the lines. It doesn't involve any free-motion stitching so is rather straightforward once you get a feel for it.

It's best to use a decorator-weight fabric such as linen or duck cotton for the pillow back, but if you are using a lightweight fabric you may need to reinforce it with light interfacing to make the fabric strong enough for the buttons and buttonholes you will stitch there.

DIFFICULTY

This project involves about 10 hours of appliqué, 8 hours of hand quilting (you can machine quilt to save time, but it won't have that cozy handmade look), and another hour or so to bind and finish the cushion. While it is not very difficult, this project involves a high level of detail as well as neat hand quilting and a piped edging on the cushion to finish.

APPLIQUÉING

1. Trace the vehicle shapes, using the templates provided, onto the paper-backed fabric adhesive; make sure the paper side is facing up. Use a separate piece of adhesive paper for each color, and trace separately whatever detail you want to appear in the contrast fabric (bumpers, door handles, wheels, and door signage panels).

Personalize the door panels by using a fabric pen to add signage, such as "Towing by Tom."

2. Leave the backing sheet on the iron-on paper adhesive and place, sticky-side down, onto the **Wrong** side of the intended fabric for each car piece; press using a hot iron. Allow the material to cool, and then cut out the appliqué design through the paper and fabric. Peel off the paper, and arrange the appliqués onto the quilt-front fabric, sticky-side down. Ends of exhaust pipes or tops of wheels will need to be tucked under the vehicle outline, and bumpers will go over vehicle outlines. Once you're sure it's all in place, press the entire shape to adhere the appliqué. When pressing, don't slide the iron around; instead, press one section firmly at a time and lift the iron onto the next section. Once everything is stuck down, go over the entire area to make sure no bits are left unstuck.

Continued from page 77

TEMPLATES
5 different cars and trucks

TECHNIQUES
Appliqué: iron-on machine appliqué
Quilting: hand quilting
Binding: piped bias binding and pillowcase method
Other: buttons and buttonholes
Hand stitches: running stitch, blanket stitch (optional)

3. Choose your thread color carefully. In some cases you will want the thread to blend in with the background fabric. With your machine set to either a medium zigzag or a blanket stitch, sew the outline of all shapes into place. Then choose a contrast color to stitch any detail such as door outlines; these are stitched using a straight stitch.

ASSEMBLING THE QUILT TOP

1. Trace your quilting grid lightly onto the background fabric. Using a water-soluble pen, make small marks 1 in/2.5 cm apart along the top and sides of the quilt. With a yardstick, connect the lines at a 45-degree angle to form a diagonal grid.

2. Draw a border around the quilt top ½ in/12 mm in from the edges; this will later be the stitching line for the piping. Make a quilt sandwich, using a quilt-basting spray to adhere the quilt top and back to the cotton batting.

3. Using a small, even running stitch, hand sew along the grid lines to the edges, being careful not to quilt over the vehicle appliqués. Tie off any thread in the selvage beyond the cushion border.

PIPING

1. If you are not turning this into a pillow, at this stage you can bind the quilt instead of attaching piping. See how to attach binding on page 41.

2. Next, you will make a continuous bias binding strip (you will need bias binding to cover the cord to make the piping; however, if you are binding it without piping, straight grain binding will be fine to use). You will want to end up with 4 yd/3.6 m of 2-in-/5-cm-wide binding strip. See page 39 for instructions on how to make a continuous bias binding strip. Then use this bias binding, following the directions on page 44 for making the piping with your cotton cord.

3. Attach the piping around the quilt top. Place the raw edge of the piped binding against the raw edges of the quilt and sew along the line you previously drew. Clip the seam allowance of the piped binding at the corners, close to the stitching line, to allow the piping to bend around the corners.

4. To join the piping, simply overlap the two pieces of cord and stitch through in a straight line. The raw ends will then be tucked and hidden away underneath when you attach the pillow back. Trim away ends.

ATTACHING THE CUSHION BACK

1. Cut your cushion back fabric into two pieces measuring 26 in/66 cm x 20 in/50.8 cm and 26 in/66 cm x 13⅟₁₆ in/34.6 cm. Fold 2.75 in/7 cm (for larger piece) and 3⅛ in/7.9 cm (for smaller piece) and press along one long side of each piece. Fold over twice for a narrow seam on the piece of fabric that will be hidden from view. Stitch each folded hem down, to provide the cushion opening. Baste the opening closed while you continue sewing, to ensure a neater finish to your cushion.

2. Place the **Right** side of the cushion cover back against the **Right** side of the quilted top and pin in place, and, following the line of stitches that you used to apply the piped binding, stitch the back cover into place.

3. To prevent the internal cushion edges from fraying during washing, you may wish to overlock or apply a zigzag stitch to the inside raw edges.

FINISHING THE QUILT

1. Turn your cushion cover **Right**-side out. Mark where the three buttonholes are to go: the first should be 1 in/2.5 cm in from the hemmed edge on the top cushion back panel in the center, and the others should be centered on either side. Use your buttons to mark how wide your buttonholes will be, and draw a line to guide you. Sew the buttonholes using your line as a guide. Some sewing machines have an automatic buttonhole stitch; if yours doesn't, don't panic. You can either hand stitch the buttonholes using a tight blanket stitch or do it manually on your sewing machine, as follows.

2. Use your zigzag stitch and set it to the smallest width (number 0.5). Set your needle position to sew on the right-hand side and stitch down that side of your marked line. Set your needle position back to the middle and change your stitch width to number 4 and sew a few stitches at the end. Then,

with needle down, and foot up, pivot your material 180 degrees. Set your needle position to sew on the other side and change your stitch width back to 0.5; stitch up the other side of the marked line. Set your needle position back to the middle and your stitch width back to number 4, sew a few back tack stitches, and you are done.

3. Cut the buttonhole open with a small pair of sharp scissors or a seam ripper, taking care not to cut into the stitching. If this is the first time you have sewn a buttonhole, make sure to practice cutting a buttonhole open on a scrap of fabric first. Then hand sew your buttons to the bottom cushion back panel, aligning them with your buttonholes.

4. Use this darling quilted cushion anywhere that kids like to sit and relax, or hang the quilt on a wall to decorate a little boy's room.

Modern Folk

Folk art is a decorative and utilitarian craft tradition that sometimes includes whimsical elements. The word folk means "of the common people," and many contemporary artists and crafters take their cue from this meaning by incorporating local lore and customs into their designs.

Sarah Steedman's Warbler Quilt uses scrap fabrics and appliqué to depict the birds that migrate each year to her backyard; Lucinda Jones's Blackbird at My Window ("Cheeky Blackbird") combines an improvised background with a quirky appliqué; Victoria Gertenbach's Grasshopper in My Garden uses a variety of stitches in her whimsical sampler; and Kellie Wulfsohn's A Little Birdie Told Me, a detailed appliqué wall hanging made for a little girl, sparks the imagination.

IN THIS SECTION:

Warbler Quilt 82 ✳ *Blackbird at My Window ("Cheeky Blackbird")* 86

Grasshopper in My Garden 90 ✳ *A Little Birdie Told Me* 96

This quilt is inspired by the flitting of small birds in and out of the backyard. The warbler is a fairly small and active bird that explores its environment before moving on. You may like to substitute a bird that is local to your area.

Warbler Quilt

by Sarah Steedman

Finished size: 13½ x 17½ in/34 x 44.5 cm

Difficulty level: **MEDIUM**

MATERIALS

¼ yd/23 cm total various scraps cotton fabric for quilt top

Cotton quilting thread

½ yd/46 cm 100 percent cotton batting

½ yd/46 cm fabric for backing

Embroidery floss in various colors

EXTRAS

Hand-sewing needles

Fabric pen

TEMPLATES

Design elements templates

TECHNIQUES

Hand stitches: whipstitch and running stitch

Appliqué: needle turn appliqué and reverse appliqué

Binding: self-binding method

NOTES

Seam allowances are all ¼ in/6 mm.

This project uses very small scraps of cotton fabric.

DIFFICULTY

This quilt has an improvised background with raw edge appliqué and heavy folk-style stitching; it is a lovely quilt to learn with and requires minimal skills in hand embroidery and appliqué.

CUTTING

1. Cut 2 pieces, each 15 x 3½ in/38 x 9 cm, from two different fabrics.

2. Cut 1 piece, 11 x 2½ in/28 x 6.5 cm. (You will cut 8 or 9 small circles into this piece of fabric before sewing down.)

3. The next pieces of fabric are cut out of any scraps of cotton you have on hand—you might want to use colors that complement each other, keep to a single-color palette, or choose colors that wildly clash:

   a. Cut one 10½-x-10-in/26.5-x-25-cm piece.

   b. Cut one 10½-x-1½-in/26.5-x-4-cm piece.

   c. Cut one 8-x-1½-in/20-x-4-cm piece.

   d. Cut one 6-x-3½-in/15-x-9-cm piece.

   e. Cut one 5½-x-3½-in/14-x-9-cm piece.

   f. Cut one 3½-x-1½-in/9-x-4-cm piece.

   g. Cut one 20½-x-16½-in/52-x-42-cm piece for the back.

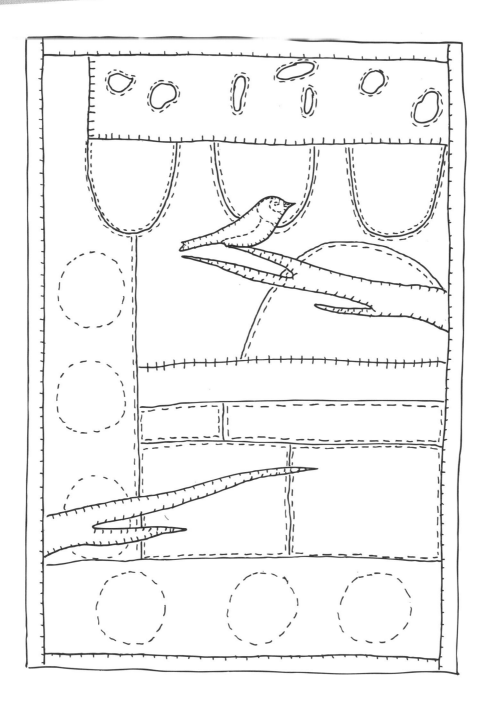

4. Trace the templates and use them to cut out the appliqué pieces in any cotton fabric you have on hand. You will cut 2 branches, a bird, a half circle, and the 3 'lobe'-shaped pieces.

ASSEMBLING THE QUILT TOP

1. Sew the quilt top with the cotton thread using the sewing diagram and iron the seams open after each is sewn, or improvise your own quilt background using fabrics you have on hand.

2. Pin the half circle to the bottom edge of the main square (the largest section; see diagram). Then attach the first thin strip to the bottom of the large piece, and sew small pieces together to make longer strips, and attach these to the bottom of the main section next. Then attach the long strip down the left of the main section and sew the strip on the bottom to finish the background of the quilt top. Press all the seams to one side.

3. Hand stitch (using a whipstitch or running stitch) the 3 'lobe' shapes down, at the top of the quilt, leaving the raw edges exposed. Take the strip that will go across the top and mark out the reverse holes with a fabric pen and cut them out. Then lay this strip across the top edge, hand stitch the raw edges down flat, and make a small running stitch around all of the small cut-out reverse appliqué circles and the lobes.

4. Lay the branch and bird shapes on the quilt top, leaving the edges raw, sew around the edges using a variety of stitches—running stitch or whipstitch, as you wish. Press the quilt top flat with a hot iron, and square up the edges.

FINISHING THE QUILT

1. Cut the batting to the same size as the quilt top.

2. Make a quilt sandwich with the three layers: quilt top (faceup), batting, and backing (facedown). Make sure an even amount of backing fabric shows all around the quilt top, with a 2-in/5-cm overhang; this will be brought to the front as a self-binding. Pin through all three layers and baste using your preferred method.

3. Hand quilt, using various colors of embroidery floss, in ⅛-in/3-mm stitches, in various patterns of your choosing. Here chunky folk-style hand quilting stitches echo the quilt squares, with the appliqué pieces as well as additional circles sewn along the bottom and side panels adding visual interest. You can add more or less quilting as you like.

4. Fold the edges of the excess backing fabric around to the quilt front, and fold the raw edge under so that there is an even ¾-in/2-cm border all around. Finish the corners square—no need to miter them. Pin as you go, then press in place to create a crisp, folded edge. Sew with small folk-style whipstitches in any color of embroidery floss you like.

This quilt shows a cheeky, chubby
raven-inspired blackbird sitting at
a window. The background has
improvisational piecing, with elements and additional embroidery
to finish.

Blackbird at My Window ("Cheeky Blackbird")

by Lucinda Jones

Finished size: approximately 16½ x 20 in/42 x 50 cm

Difficulty level:  **MEDIUM**

MATERIALS

- ½ yd/46 cm total various green cotton quilting fabrics for background and lighter green for window frames and dividers
- ¼ yd/23 cm cotton for binding
- Small piece black brushed cotton for the bird
- Small piece brown fabric for the branch
- Any small scraps fabric for the appliquéd leaves
- Cotton quilting thread in coordinating colors, including off-white
- ½ yd/46 cm cotton for backing
- ½ yd/46 cm cotton batting
- Pearl cotton thread for embroidery in green, brown, yellow, and black
- Small, shiny black glass bead for the eye

EXTRAS

- Paper
- Ruler
- Rotary cutter and cutting mat
- Tailor's chalk (optional)
- Embroidery or darning foot for free-motion stitching
- Hand-sewing needles, size 10 quilting needle, and a larger needle for the pearl cotton

TEMPLATES

- Blackbird body, tail, wing
- Leaves

List continues next page

NOTES

Seam allowances are all ¼ in/6 mm unless otherwise indicated.

Choose a lighter-colored fabric for the window frame and to go behind the bird legs, in order to highlight these areas.

Press the seams in toward the window frame, raising this area and making it appear three-dimensional.

The background uses improvisational piecing; you will need a ruler, rotary cutter, and cutting mat. If you don't have these, you can use a ruler and pencil to mark a line, and trim using high-quality fabric scissors.

DIFFICULTY

This quilt is of moderate difficulty. Piecing the background using improvisation is fun; however, it includes some appliqué, embroidery, and freestyle quilting that requires a bit of practice.

CUTTING

1. Cut four window frame pieces, two (10¾-x-1½-in/27.5-x-4-cm) pieces, and two (11-x-1½-in/28-x-4-cm) pieces from a fabric lighter than the background fabric

2. Cut four window panes: 3½-x-4½-in/9-x-11-cm pieces

3. Cut three window dividers: two 1-x-4½-in/2.5-x-11.5-cm pieces, and one 1-x-7-in/2.5-x-17-cm piece

4. Cut strips of fabric for binding, each 2 in/5 cm wide and long enough to go around the perimeter of the quilt. Please see page 39 for directions on how to cut continuous straight binding.

5. Trace and cut templates from paper.

6. Cut one bird body, wing, and tail from black brushed cotton.

7. Cut out improvised branch from brown cotton. (Use illustration on page 89 as a guide.)

8. Cut five leaf shapes from five different fabric scraps.

MAKING YOUR WINDOW

1. Sew the top two windowpanes, with one shorter center divider strip in between. Then sew the bottom windowpanes with the second shorter center divider strip in between. Press the seams toward the window divider strips, raising the window frames for a slightly three-dimensional effect.

2. Mark the center of the long window divider strip, using that mark to line up the center of each pane. Join the top panes and the bottom panes together and press. Then use your ruler, rotary cutter, and cutting mat to square up the sides of the window.

Continued from page 87

TECHNIQUES

Piecing: improvisational piecing

Quilting: free-motion machine quilting

Appliqué: Needle turn appliqué

Hand stitches: back stitch, running stitch, and satin stitch

Binding: mitered binding

3. Sew the long window frame sides to the window-pane section with the cotton thread. Press, then trim the edges straight and the corners square. Then sew on the top and bottom window frame pieces and square up corners. Press seams toward the window frame pieces.

IMPROVISATIONAL PIECING

1. From the green fabric for the background, cut the fabric piece for above the window at least 9 x 2½ in/ 23 x 6 cm, and sew onto the top of the window. Use a ruler and rotary cutter to trim the edges even with the width of the window section.

2. Next, cut a fabric piece for placing at the right side of the window, at least 1¾ x 13 in/4.5 x 33 cm. Again, use your ruler and rotary cutter to trim the edges even with the previous section. Add a fabric piece, at least 3½ x 13 in/9 x 33 cm, to the right of the window section and trim square. Continue adding pieces, from your green background fabrics, in this way, around the window, trimming to size as you go, squaring up the corners and edges.

3. Continue to use improvisational piecing for the strips underneath the window frame. Sew on a strip, press, and then square up the corners and edges. Sew small pieces together to form strips first if you wish; press seams and then sew onto the main section. Feel free to place the various fabrics at angles and use fabrics that echo those used around and in the window frame. Use lighter colors in the center to highlight where the bird legs will be placed.

4. When you are happy with the size, square up the entire quilt top and press.

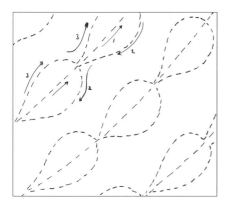

FINISHING THE QUILT

1. Cut the backing and batting 1 in/2.5 cm larger on each side than the quilt top, and make a quilt sandwich. Baste with your preferred method and machine quilt using a freestyle design. Here a leaf motif was used; however, you can use any freestyle design you like. See tips on page 38 and draw your design on the quilt top first using tailor's chalk.

2. Pin the bird motif onto the quilt top, and appliqué the bird body following the instructions for "pinch and turn" appliqué on page 24. Leave an opening for the tail. Slide in the tail and pin, and then appliqué and finish sewing the body. Attach the wing into position using the same method.

3. Pin the branch into position, using the diagram provided, and appliqué the branch, again using the "pinch and turn" method. Embroider small branches and leaves onto one end of the branch if desired, using a back stitch, with embroidery thread in greens and brown. Appliqué the leaf motifs, using the "pinch and turn" method, in a straight line at the top of the quilt. Add a line of running stitch down the center of each leaf.

4. Embroider the legs in two steps. First, outline the leg shape using backstitch in brown thread.

Then use yellow thread to overlay this line in a very loose satin stitch, adding claws at the toes.

5. Use black cotton thread to sew a running stitch along the sides of the legs and toes. Use off-white cotton quilting thread to outline the bird body, wing, and tail with a running stitch close to the edge of the appliquéd pieces. Add the mouth and eye with the same thread; sew on the bead for the eye.

6. Using the fabric you have cut for the binding, make up enough continuous binding to go around your quilt, and then attach using the traditional binding method with mitered corners, shown on page 41.

7. Add a label and a hanging sleeve (see page 45) to the back, and you are done.

The life and activity in the garden inspired this quilt—which has the feel of a hot summer day with various creatures, each busy doing their own thing. This adorable quilt is constructed using a variety of small pieces of cotton fabric, and it is brought to life with a lot of hand-embroidered stitches, which are used in place of traditional quilting stitches.

Grasshopper in My Garden

by Victoria Gertenbach

Finished size: 17½ x 10 in/44.5 x 25 cm

Difficulty level: **MEDIUM**

MATERIALS

¼ yd/23 cm total various 100 percent cotton fabrics for quilt top

Cotton quilting thread

¼ yd/23 cm cotton fabric for binding

12 x 24 in/30 x 60 cm fabric for backing

12 x 24 in/30 x 60 cm thin quilt batting

Embroidery floss in 5 assorted colors

3 small buttons and 1 medium button

EXTRAS

12 x 24 in/30 x 60 cm iron-on stabilizer (optional)

Acid-free glue (optional)

Iron-on transfer pencil, carbon paper, or tissue paper

TEMPLATE

Grasshopper

TECHNIQUES

Appliqué: machine appliqué

Quilting: machine quilting "stitch in the ditch" method

Binding: mitered corner binding

Hand stitches: running stitch, backstitch, straight stitch, cross-stitch, and French knots

NOTES

Seam allowances are all ¼ in/6 mm, unless otherwise indicated.

Press seams to the left after sewing each section.

All appliqué pieces have their raw edges turned under ¼ in/6 mm. The edges are then tacked in place before machine stitching onto the quilt top. After the edges have been turned and hand stitched, press with a hot iron.

Wash and iron all fabric before beginning this project.

DIFFICULTY

Because this project has relatively simple machine piecing and appliqué, not much experience is required, but you will need to do quite a bit of hand sewing and embroidery, as well as a traditional mitered binding.

CUTTING

1. Cut out the fabric using the diagram provided:

    a. Sections #1 and #3: 18 x 2½ in/46 x 6 cm

    b. Section #2 is made up of 4 pieces:

    #2a + #2d: 4¾ x 2½ in/12 x 6 cm

    #2b: 4¾ x 5½ in/12 x 14 cm

    #2c: 4¾ x 8¾ in/12 x 22 cm

    c. Section #4: 18 x 2 in/46 x 5 cm

2. Cut out the appliqué pieces:

    a. 2-in-/5-cm-diameter circle for the large flower

    b. 5-x-1½-in/12.5-x-4-cm rectangle for the flower stem

    c. 3-x-2-in/7.5-x-5-cm leaf shape, drawn freehand

    d. 3½-in-/9-cm-diameter circle for the sun, cut in half

    e. 4 small squares and rectangles ranging in size from a 1½-in/4-cm square to a 1½-x-2½-in/4-x-6-cm rectangle

    f. 7½-x-1½-in/19-cm-x-4-cm strip

3. Cut fabric for binding: 2¾ in wide x 60 in long/6 cm x 1.5 m

---

ASSEMBLING THE QUILT TOP

1. The actual quilt-top background is super-simple. Sew the four pieces in section #2 together in a strip and press; then sew section #1 to section #2 and add sections #3 and #4, and press the quilt top.

2. The two appliqué pieces—the sun at the top of the quilt and a small square at the bottom—have an edge that lies along the outside of the quilt. Leave this edge unturned when appliquéing.

3. If you wish, iron a piece of stabilizer onto the back of the quilt top. This gives the quilt top a bit more stability when you are appliquéing the pieces.

4. Prepare the appliqué pieces by turning under the seam allowances and pressing to create neat edges. To do this with the flower circle, use a paper template with a smaller diameter than that of the circle; sew a loose running stitch around the outside edge, then gently gather in the edges around the paper template and press the seam allowance down to create a neat round edge. With the half circle, clip the curved edge, carefully turn under, and press as you go to create a neat, rounded curve.

5. Then place all the appliqué pieces onto the quilt top, using the diagram as a guide, and pin into position around the edges (you may use acid-free glue here that will wash out later).

6. With matching thread, use either a simple zigzag stitch or something more decorative to machine stitch the motifs to the quilt top.

7. Transfer the grasshopper design onto section #2c, using either an iron-on transfer pencil or carbon paper. Alternatively, you could trace the design onto tissue paper and sew through the paper, tearing it away as you finish each section.

FINISHING THE QUILT

1. Remove the stabilizer from the quilt back (if you used it) and make a quilt sandwich with your backing, batting, and quilt top (see page 33). Baste the three layers together using your preferred basting method.

2. The first bit of quilting is done using the "stitch in the ditch" method (see page 38). Sew directly over the seam lines, invisibly joining all the layers together. First sew all the seam lines, and then sew around the perimeter of each appliquéd piece.

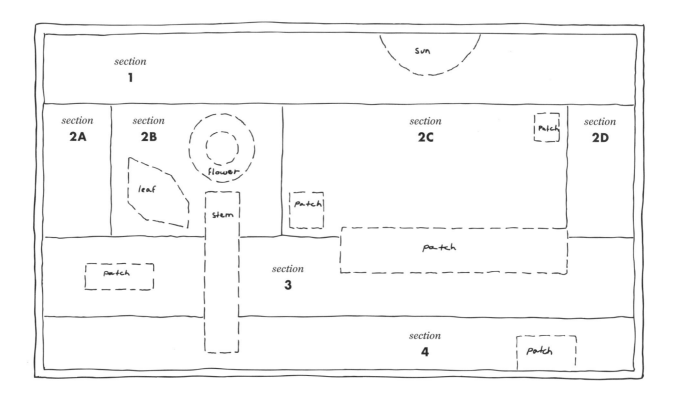

3. You'll use a variety of simple embroidery stitches in finishing the quilt. Feel free to use as many or as few as you like. This is a perfect opportunity to unleash your creativity and practice your stitches. Use the fabric you have chosen to guide your choices. Use 3 strands of floss for the stitches, except where noted, and use the diagram to show you where to place your stitches.

a. Backstitch: The grasshopper is completed using backstitch. Use 6 strands of embroidery floss for the chest area and back leg and thigh area, and 3 strands for the remaining areas. Here, black embroidery floss has been used, but feel free to use any color as long as it contrasts with the background.

b. More backstitches are used for the stems of the little flowers in section #3, for the random half circles in section #4, and for the sun's rays. Small crosses are made using backstitch at the bottom of the flower stem appliqué and at the far right of section #3.

c. Running stitch: The inside of the sun, the appliqué circle, and around the inside edges of section #3 are completed using a running stitch.

d. Straight stitch: The main two center sections, #2b and #2c, have randomly placed straight stitches, or seed stitches, all over.

e. Cross-stitch: Use small- and medium-sized cross-stitches, randomly placed in sections #1, #3, and #4 and inside the long rectangle appliqué beneath the grasshopper.

f. French knots: These are made with 6 strands of embroidery floss and are placed at regular intervals in the outside center sections #2a and #2d, and to make the small flowers in section #3.

4. Trim and square the edges of the quilt and bind the quilt using the traditional binding method described on page 41. Attach a hanging sleeve to the back of the quilt as described in the instructions on page 45. After completing the stitches, sew your decorative buttons in place, using the illustration on page 95 as a guide.

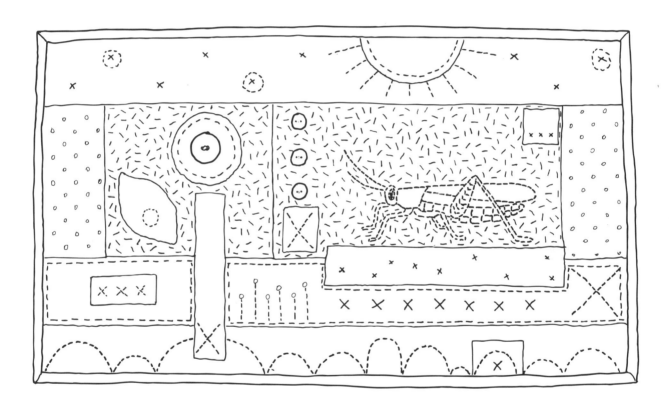

This quilt is perfectly sized to hang over a little girl's bed. You can easily manipulate the design to create an altogether different scene, allowing for endless design possibilities.

A Little Birdie Told Me

by Kellie Wulfsohn

Finished size: 38 x 25½ in/96.5 x 65 cm

Difficulty level: **TRICKY**

MATERIALS

¾ yd/68.5 cm white cotton for quilt top fabric

1 yd x 45 in/91 x 114 cm fabric for backing in green print or multiple scraps different greens

31 in x 43 in/79 x 109 cm cotton high-loft batting

⅓ yd/30.5 cm coordinating striped fabric for binding

⅓ yd/30.5 cm total various scraps for appliqué shapes

Thread in coordinating colors, including white, for hand and machine sewing

1 yd/91 cm fabric for backing and hanging sleeve

EXTRAS

Fusible web

Fine-tip permanent marker

Water-soluble fabric spray-on starch

Basting glue or basting spray

Water-soluble fabric pen

Embroidery or darning foot for free-motion stitching

Safety pins

Quilting gloves (optional)

TEMPLATES

Flowers, leaves, birds, ladybug, and butterfly appliqué shapes

3 of #1a and #1b (tulip-shaped flowers)

5 of #2 (square-edged flower petals)

8 of #3 (rounded flower petals)

1 of #4 and 3 of #4 in reverse

NOTES

Seam allowances are all ¼ in/6 mm.

All materials used are quilting cottons.

The appliqué is applied with fusible web and secured using a machine blanket stitch.

All flower stems are ⅜-in/1-cm bias strips that have been attached by hand. If you wish, you could instead choose to use a green rickrack braid, or even fuse the stems and blanket stitch their edges, similar to the edges of other appliqué shapes.

All of the stitching detail shown here was achieved using free-motion machine stitching. You could achieve a similar result with fabric markers and a steady hand, followed by machine stitching along the lines made by the fabric marker. However, I would recommend that you try this first on a scrap of fabric to ensure that you will be happy with the results.

Wear quilting gloves while machine quilting to assist with smooth movement of the quilt under the machine. You may also like to practice on a small sample of quilt sandwich prior to starting on your actual quilt. Practicing quilting on a sample beforehand will also help you make sure that the settings on your machine are correct.

DIFFICULTY

This quilt is a little bit challenging, with lots of tricky cutting and machine appliqué, as well as free-motion machine quilting, however the design is flexible and fun to do.

List continues next page

CUTTING:

1. Cut 1 (30-x-42-in/76-x-106.5-cm) rectangle from white quilt top fabric.

2. Cut 1 (31-x-43-in/79-x-109-cm) rectangle from the backing fabric and batting.

3. Cut a total of 7 yds/6.4 m of ⅜-in-/1-cm-wide bias strips using the green fabrics.

4. Cut 4 (2¼-in/5-cm) strips from the striped fabric, along the cross grain of the fabric, for the binding. (This allows ample excess for the matching of stripes).

5. Use some of the backing fabric to make a 3-in/7.5-cm hanging sleeve (see page 45).

PREPARING THE APPLIQUÉ

1. Prepare the quilt top fabric by first ensuring that it is squared. Press. Fold the quilt top fabric in half horizontally and finger press. Repeat this process, folding the fabric vertically. Open your fabric and lay it on a flat surface. You now have your center lines marked, providing you with registration points that will assist with placement of your appliqué.

2. Always follow the manufacturer's directions regarding the use of your fusible web. Trace the appliqué template shapes onto the backing paper of the fusible web using a permanent marker, ensuring that you leave adequate space between, and a small margin around, each of your shapes, to allow them to be separated.

3. Separate all of the shapes; don't cut too closely around them just yet (see template pieces listed), and, with your various fabric scraps that you will use to make the appliqué motifs, select the color combinations that you intend to use. Adhere the fusible web to the **Wrong** side of the fabric pieces using your iron, following the manufacturer's instructions.

4. Now, cut out the fabric shapes and match up the pieces to be layered: flowers (numbers 1, 2, 3, and 5), the two birds (#7), the 9 ladybugs (#8), and the butterfly (#13). Remove the backing paper from the appliqué shapes to reveal the tacky surface of the fusible web. Using the photograph as a guide,

---

Continued from page 97

13 of #5 (circle flower centers to go with numbers 2 and 3)

9 of #6 (small bell flowers)

1 of #7a and 1 of #7a in reverse (bird body)

1 of #7b and 1 of #7b in reverse (bird wing)

9 of #8a and 9 of #8b (ladybugs' wings and body)

5 of #9 and 5 of #9 in reverse (shorter leaves)

6 of #10 (long leaves)

3 of #11 (leaves)

12 of #12 (square-edge leaves)

1 of #13a and #13b (butterfly)

TECHNIQUES

Appliqué: iron-on machine stitch appliqué and needle turn appliqué

Hand stitches: blind stitch

Quilting: free-motion machine quilting

Binding: mitered corner binding

roughly set out the appliqué shapes. Do not spend a lot of time on this task, because you are likely to move them around quite a lot before they are finally ironed into place.

5. Make the stems of the flowers from the green ⅜-in/ 1-cm bias strips. The tallest flower stems should be approximately 22 in/56 cm and the shortest should be approximately 4 in/10 cm. Cut the lengths, leaving yourself a couple of inches of overhang to allow for adjustment if required.

6. Using a hot iron and a small amount of spray starch, you will be able to create the gentle curves of the stems. Once you have all of the pieces on the background fabric, stand back and make sure that you are happy with the overall design. Once you are satisfied, use a small amount of basting glue along the length of each stem to temporarily hold the stems in place. Now, iron the appliqué shapes in place using a hot iron with no steam.

7. Hand stitch the stems in place using a blind stitch.

8. Using a water-soluble fabric pen and the photograph as a reference, mark out the embroidery stitching detail on the quilt top: butterfly and ladybug feelers, curlicues, bird tails, legs, and beaks.

APPLIQUÉING

1. Sandwich the quilt top and batting together and spray baste; do not attach the backing fabric at this point. This allows you to match your top thread to your bobbin thread without worrying about matching it to your backing fabric. It also eliminates the need to use a tear-away stabilizer.

2. Using a thread that matches the appliqué shape you will be working on, do a machine blanket stitch around the edges of all of the fused appliqué shapes (a small zigzag stitch will suffice if your machine does not have a blanket stitch). Pull the loose threads at the rear of the fabric and tie them off.

MACHINE EMBROIDERY

1. Change your machine foot to a free-motion foot and drop your feed dogs (see page 15 for more information on how to do this). Select a top and bobbin thread to complement the stitching detail that you intend to complete.

2. Begin by lowering your needle into the quilt an inch or so from the shape. Raise the needle and pull on the top thread, pulling the bobbin thread through to the top. Lower and raise the needle again temporarily, securing the two threads on the top of the quilt. Slide your quilt to your intended starting point and lower your needle. Free-motion stitch over the marked line several times until the row of stitching has the thickness you desire. When you are completing spots on the ladybug, first sew a small circle, and sew vertically and then horizontally over the area until the space is entirely filled with stitches.

3. Take several stitches close together at the start and finish points of each appliqué shape. This will secure the stitching, allowing you to cut the threads at the quilt surface so you don't need to bury threads.

FINISHING THE QUILT

1. Complete a quilt sandwich by pin basting or spray basting the backing fabric to the quilt top and batting section. Once this step is complete, stitch

just outside the edges of all of the appliqué shapes using a white thread, to match your background fabric. Next, complete the background quilting. You might like to use the quilting design shown here, or any free-motion scribble or stipple design. You might like to use quilting gloves while completing this work, since there is quite a bit to do. (See page 38 for more detailed instructions on free-motion machine quilting.)

2. Trim the quilt to its finished size, ensuring that the corners are square and sides are even and straight. Make a hanging sleeve with a strip of fabric that is 5½ in/14 cm wide and the length of the quilt, and add it to the back.

3. Join the binding strips, matching the stripes. Press your binding once down the center, lengthwise. Bind the quilt following the instructions on page 41 for double-fold binding with mitered corners. Add a label, and you are finished!

Modern Elegance

Elegance, a study in subtlety and grace, always shows restraint, is balanced and neat, and has an ingenious simplicity. The quilts in this section use natural fabrics and a limited color palette paired with simple designs and very few decorative elements, creating pattern in a clever way.

My Shibori Sampler quilt uses an ancient Japanese dye method to experiment with pattern; Alexandra Rasmussen's Blattwerk quilt features a simple, repeating pattern, resulting in a subtle textured design; Meg Spaeth's Power-line Sky quilt takes a perspective line drawing and turns it into an experiment in color; and the Concentric Circles lap quilt by Alison Brookbanks uses space to emphasize the intricate layers of circles.

IN THIS SECTION:

Shibori Sampler 102 * *Blattwerk* 106

Power-line Sky 110 * *Concentric Circles* 114

This quilt uses a very simple piecing technique—the nine patch, combined with an ancient Japanese dyeing method, Shibori "fold and clamp." All the squares used in the quilt are experiments, or samples, of this method of dyeing fabric. Be forewarned— the element of chance in creating these patterns is addictive, and once you have made one of these it is very difficult to stop.

Shibori Sampler

by Kathreen Ricketson

Finished size: 16 in/40.5 cm square

Difficulty level: **EASY**

MATERIALS

- ½ yd/46 cm white medium-weight 100 percent cotton fabric
- Clips, clamps, and pegs and small flat blocks of wood in various shapes
- Fabric dye
- Cotton quilting thread
- 17-in/43-cm square 100 percent cotton batting
- 17-in/43-cm square 100 percent cotton fabric for backing
- Embroidery thread

EXTRAS

- Iron
- Rubber gloves
- Plastic sheet for workbench
- Tailor's chalk
- Plates, bowls, or glasses
- Quilting hoop

TECHNIQUES

- Decorative elements: Shibori "fold and clamp" dyeing method
- Binding: pillowcase method
- Hand stitches: slip stitch and running stitch or whipstitch.
- Quilting: hand quilting

NOTES

Seam allowances are all ¼ in/6 mm.

Be sure to read and follow the instructions on your dye packet carefully and use appropriate safety equipment for the type of dye you are using.

Darker dye colors on white cotton give greater contrast and create more obvious patterns.

Use rubber gloves to save your skin, and use an old saucepan for the dye bath.

Ironing when folding the fabric creates crisp edges to your design.

DIFFICULTY

Though the sewing required for this quilt is easy, the Shibori dye method will probably take a bit of experimenting before you get a result that pleases you (or you might be lucky the first time around). You will use the pillowcase binding method, and some hand quilting is involved, but only as much as you can handle.

FOLDING AND DYEING

1. Cut out twelve 6-in/15-cm squares of white fabric. (You will only use nine in your final quilt, but it is handy to make extras in case you make a mistake, and also to allow for additional choices at the end.

2. Take one square at a time and fold each one using a variation of the Shibori folding and clamping technique (see page 27). Fold and iron as you go to achieve crisp color edges. Use small wooden blocks as resist shapes clamped to your folded sections for more design options.

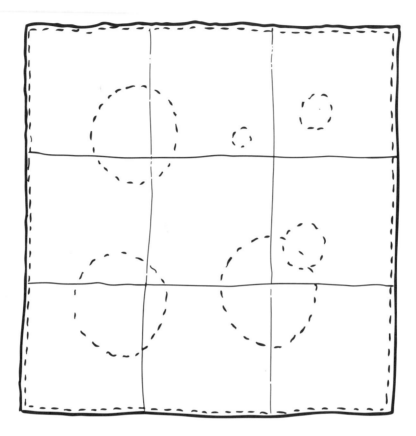

3. Make up your dye bath using the instructions on your dye packet. Black dye was used in this quilt.

4. Wearing rubber gloves, dip the edges of the folded fabric in the dye bath for just a few seconds. The longer the fabric stays in the dye, the more dye will bleed into the fabric. You may want to dip the whole piece in the dye bath or only dip one edge in; you may have to do this a few times to get it right as you get to know the dye solution you are using.

5. Untie and unclamp the fabric samples. Don't rinse straightaway; instead, lay the pieces out flat on your plastic sheet and leave for about 20 minutes before rinsing them out in warm soapy water. Rinse again in cold water until the water runs clear. Dry by either hanging them on a rack or putting them in the dryer for 10 minutes. Press flat. You may need to trim and square up the edges.

ASSEMBLING THE QUILT TOP

1. Choose nine of your squares of dyed fabric. Move them around and work out your preferred composition for your final nine-patch quilt.

2. Sew the squares, **Right** sides together, with the cotton thread, one at a time, creating three rows of three squares. Iron the seams open—this will help you when you are aligning the squares. Then sew the rows together, being careful to line up the squares so that the seams match up exactly. Press the seams open, and trim the edges if required.

- -

FINISHING THE QUILT

1. Cut out a piece of batting and a piece of backing fabric the same size as your finished quilt top. (Use 100 percent cotton batting and backing so that it is completely machine washable.)

2. Put the layers together using the instructions for the pillowcase method on page 41, and sew around the edges, leaving an opening of about 6 in/15 cm on one side. Turn it **Right**-side out through the opening, using a chopstick to push the corners out. Press carefully around the edges. Hand sew the opening closed using a slip stitch.

3. Use a running stitch to hand quilt around the whole quilt about ½ in/12 mm from the edge.

4. Draw circles in various shapes, using tailor's chalk, on the back of the quilt, by tracing around plates, bowls, or glasses.

5. Lay the quilt out flat and press smooth. Without basting, place the first section to be quilted in a quilting hoop, tighten up the screw until just taut, and hand quilt around the circles using a small running stitch. A contrasting embroidery thread would give a stunning effect, or, as I have done, you could use a neutral color so the quilting does not compete with the fabric design.

6. For a time, I was addicted to making these, and with the help of my two children I made enough to use as place mats; since they are completely machine washable this is a perfect use for them. You can do this or just make one (or several) to hang on your wall. If you are hanging them, you will want to attach a hanging sleeve (see page 45) to the back.

This quilt is a celebration of subtle color and texture, incorporating scraps of woolen fabric arranged in a delightful and simple leaf motif that can be adapted to all sorts of projects. This quilt is a nine-patch design with the repetition of a woolen leaf motif (*Blattwerk* is a German term for a leaf or foliage design motif) on each block; the colors you use should reflect your mood or the season of the year.

Blattwerk

by Alexandra Rasmussen

Finished size: 19 x 20 in/48 x 50 cm

Difficulty level: **MEDIUM**

MATERIALS

⅓ yd/30.5 cm total various small pieces of leftover or recycled wool fabrics

½ yd/46 cm linen for quilt top

2¼ yd/2 m (3-in-/7.5-cm-wide) binding (You can make your own binding using the same fabric as the backing. Or you may like to piece some scraps of fabric together, to give some interest to the binding.)

⅝ yd/57 cm fabric for backing (Or you can piece your backing from smaller pieces of fabric like those used in this quilt.)

21 x 22 in/53.5 x 56 cm thin cotton batting

Cotton quilting thread

EXTRAS

⅓ yd/30.5 cm thin iron-on fusible interfacing

Scissors

Cardboard

Fray-check spray (in case the woolen leaf motifs look like they might fray too much)

TEMPLATE

Leaf design template

TECHNIQUES

Quilting: machine quilting and hand quilting

Binding: mitered corner binding

Appliqué: machine raw edge appliqué

Hand stitches: running stitch

NOTES

Seam allowances are all ¼ in/6 mm.

If you are using the finished piece as a decorative wall hanging, you do not need to prewash the fabric.

The leaf block can easily be transformed into various other projects, such as coasters, pillow covers, curtains, and an embellishment on a front pocket of an apron. Use wool if you do not plan to wash the item often; cotton or linen can also be used to make the leaf motif.

The size of this project is flexible—make more blocks or increase the size of the blocks for larger items such as blankets or coverlets.

DIFFICULTY

This project is not difficult, but one must work with care. Using very coarsely woven heavyweight wool fabrics will increase the difficulty of the project. Instead, you can use more finely woven medium-weight wool fabrics to avoid trouble with fraying open edges.

CUTTING

1. Cut about twenty-five 2-x-10-in/5-x-25-cm strips from a variety of medium-weight wools. You can vary the width of the strips, but keep them all 10 in/25 cm long, and note that you may need to cut a slightly different number of strips.

2. Cut nine 6½-x-7-in/16.5-x-17.5-cm linen rectangles.

3. Cut enough 3-in-/7.5-cm-wide strips to go around the outside for the binding.

MAKING THE LEAF MOTIFS

1. Assemble the wool strips according to how you want the leaves to be colored and sew **Right** sides together, making five sheets of different-colored stripes.

2. Press seams open with steam. Weight them down while you are letting them cool (use something heavy like a few big books for about 10 minutes) to get really flat seams. Then, on the **Wrong** side of the striped sheets, iron on light interfacing to make sure the seams stay flat.

3. Trace the leaf template onto cardboard, and use it to cut nine shapes out of the sheets of sewn woolen strips. Then cut the shapes in half lengthwise (see illustration below). At this stage, you can mix and match the leaf halves to get combinations you like. Put them together in pairs ready to appliqué onto the quilt top. Spray edges with fray-check spray at this point if you think the wool is going to fray excessively.

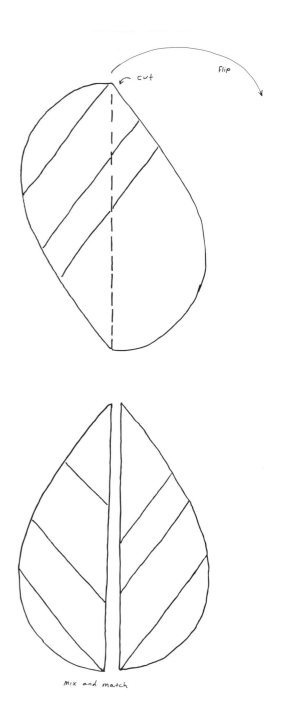

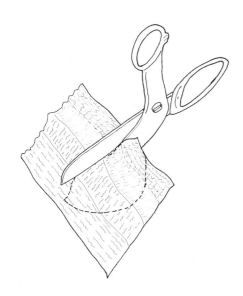

mix and match

ASSEMBLING THE QUILT

1. Sew the linen squares together in a simple nine-patch design—three rows of three squares each—making sure to line up the seams exactly.

2. For your backing you can use one whole piece of fabric or piece it together from scraps. Then cut out both the backing fabric and batting 1 in/2.5 cm larger on all sides than your quilt top.

3. Prepare a quilt sandwich and baste together using your preferred method.

4. Hand quilt one line of small stitches, using cotton thread, ¼ in/6 mm inside each square, echoing the seam line, starting with the center square. Then trim and square up the edges of the quilt.

5. Measure the perimeter of the quilt and add 6 in/15 cm (for overlapping when bringing the ends together). Make your double-fold binding using the fabric you cut earlier. Attach the binding with a mitered corner using the binding instructions on page 41.

6. Place one half of a woolen leaf in the center of each square, aligned on the diagonal, and pin into place. Starting at the bottom, machine sew, with cotton thread, in the direction of the tip on the center line, then sew the outer edge. Don't cut the thread; instead, leave the needle in the fabric while you align and pin the second half of the leaf close to the edge of the first half.

7. Proceed with topstitching. Then, without cutting the thread, quilt the inner part of the leaves as shown on the diagram. Repeat with the other eight leaves and you have yourself a beautiful textured leaf quilt perfect for all seasons. Attach a hanging sleeve (see page 45) to finish.

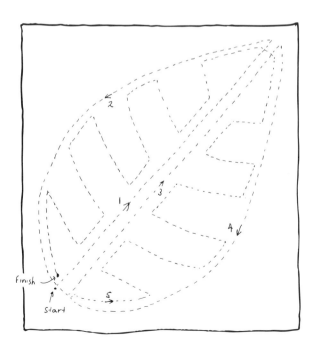

This quilt embraces our modern landscape, using power lines cutting across the sky to create a patchwork design. There are a couple of variations to this quilt, a one-piece design for those interested in simplicity (for this, simply use the design to embroider on plain cloth), and a vivid patchwork piece combining neutral cottons with aqua and orange for a surreal effect (the instructions for which are described in the method). Don't worry about straight seams or wonky quilting; this landscape isn't perfect, but that's what makes it beautiful.

Power-line Sky

by Meg Spaeth

Finished size: 11 x 16 in/28 x 40.5 cm

Difficulty level: **TRICKY**

MATERIALS

¼ yd/23 cm total various cotton prints and solids, for the pieced background quilt or 11½ x 16½ in/29 x 42 cm fabric for solid quilt top

Small pieces of brown wool felt or white wool felt

13 x 18 in/33 x 46 cm fabric for backing

13 x 18 in/33 x 46 cm flannel for batting

Cotton quilting thread

1¾ yds/1.6 m (⅛-in/3-mm-diameter) cotton cord for piping

3½ yd/3.2 m premade single-fold bias tape in a neutral color

Embroidery floss

EXTRAS

Freezer paper

Iron

Tailor's chalk (optional)

Iron-on transfer pencil

Drinking glass

Zipper foot

TEMPLATE

Whole quilt pattern

TECHNIQUES

Piecing: curved piecing

Quilting: "stitch in the ditch" method

Appliqué: minimal raw-edge appliqué

Hand stitches: whipstitch, backstitch, running stitch, and slip stitch

Binding: bias binding and piped binding

NOTES

Seam allowances are all ¼ in/6 mm.

There are nineteen pieces for this quilt, all of them different, so it is important to pin your pattern pieces to your cut fabric or number your cut pieces with chalk.

As you read the directions and piece this quilt together, always consult the sketch for placement.

Press the seam allowances to the right after they are sewn together. However, if the seam allowance will show through, then press toward the darker piece.

If making the solid one-piece quilt top, use the pattern pieces as a guide to draw on the quilting lines with tailor's chalk and skip ahead to the quilting and embroidery step.

DIFFICULTY

Because there are so many pieces and they are assembled in a certain order, this project requires attention. Piped binding is used for finishing off, and it can be tricky if you have not done it before.

CUTTING

1. Use the template to trace your pattern pieces onto freezer paper and label the pattern pieces. Iron the templates onto your chosen fabrics.

2. Cut pieces 1 to 17 from quilting cotton and 18 and 19 from wool felt. Put aside the felt pieces (these are the telephone poles and will be used last).

ASSEMBLING THE QUILT TOP

1. To begin, sew pieces 1, 2, and 3 together; this will make the upper part of the quilt top. Next, sew pieces 4 and 5 together to make the middle piece.

2. To begin making the right corner piece, carefully pin pieces 7 and 8 together along the curved edge, sew, and clip the seam allowance along the curve. Attach the straight side that is composed of 7 and 8 to piece 6. Now sew pieces 13 and 14 to the bottom of this piece.

3. Next, sew pieces 15, 16, and 17 together and attach to 14, completing the right corner piece. Last, sew pieces 9, 10, 11, and 12 together to finish the left corner piece.

4. Now you should have four large pieces: the upper piece, the middle piece, the bottom right corner, and bottom left corner.

5. Assemble the 4 large pieces together, by sewing the middle piece to the bottom right corner piece. Then join this piece to the top piece, making sure to match the seams. Finally, fit the bottom left corner by sewing it to the piece above and then the piece to the right of it. Press the entire quilt top.

QUILTING AND EMBROIDERY

1. Lay the backing fabric **Right**-side down. Place the flannel (used in place of batting) on top, and then put the quilt top on the flannel **Right**-side up. Baste or pin the quilt sandwich together.

2. Quilt using the "stitch in the ditch" method along the seam lines with a machine or by hand (see page 38). The quilting will create the telephone wires, so be sure to use contrasting thread so the stitching will show up.

3. Pin pieces 18 and 19 in place and hand sew them onto the background using a whipstitch.

4. Transfer the design using an iron-on transfer pencil or draw the support poles for the telephone lines freehand onto your quilt top and embroider them using a backstitch. Square up the quilt so it measures 11½ x 16½ in/29 x 42 cm.

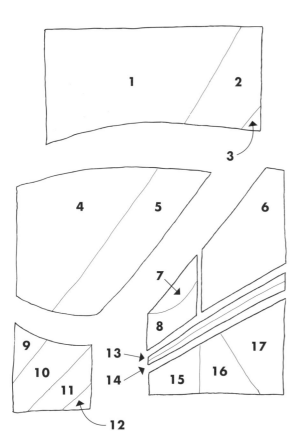

FINISHING THE QUILT

1. This quilt uses a piped binding that is made in two stages: first the piping is made and attached, and then the single-fold binding is sewn over this. Doing this in stages helps to keep the piping in place so it doesn't move around inside the binding and holds it snug against the edge of the quilt.

2. To create rounded corners, place a drinking glass on the quilt as close to the corner as possible, without it going off the edge, and trace the curve onto the quilt. Do this for each of the corners and trim.

3. To make the piping, take 1¾ yd/1.6 m of the premade single-fold bias tape and iron it out flat to remove the folds (or make your own bias tape, see page 39), then fold it in half lengthwise and press. Fit the piping cord into the crease and use a zipper foot to machine sew down the length of the folded bias tape, as close as you can to the cord (see page 44 for more detailed instructions). Leave a few inches open at one end.

4. Take the remaining 1¾ yd/1.6 m of bias tape and line up one raw edge of the tape with the raw edge of the quilt top, and pin into place all around. Then place the encased piping on top of the bias tape, matching all the raw edges. Pin all the way around. You will be sewing the piping to the quilt at the same time as one side of the binding and then folding the binding over the piping in order to encase the piping inside the binding.

5. Still using the zipper foot, sew all the layers together, staying as close to the piping cord as you can and stopping a few inches short of where the ends meet.

6. When you come to the end, first mark where the bias tape will meet, and cut the bias tape, leaving a ¼-in/6-mm seam allowance. With **Right** sides facing, sew together.

7. Inside of the open end of the piped binding tape, cut off 1 in/2.5 cm or so of the piping cord. Trim the other end of the piping so it butts up against the cut end, and fit the flap of the bias tape over it (see page 44 for joining ends of piping). Pin and sew.

8. Wrap the outer bias tape over the piping, to the back of the quilt. The piping and all the raw edges should now be enclosed in the binding. Pin the binding onto the back of the quilt, and then hand stitch into place using a slip stitch.

9. This surreal landscape is perfect as a wall hanging. You may want to put it inside a frame or attach a hanging sleeve (see page 45) to the back of it.

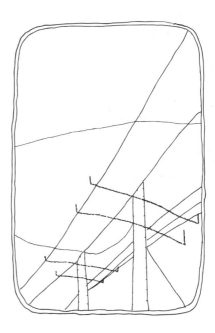

This crib quilt, lap quilt, or play mat uses natural linen as a base for a series of concentric circles in contrasting fabrics that accordion inward to create a textured landscape. These can be pulled, shaped, and explored by small hands and fingers, or just admired for their colors, textures, and patterns. Sashiko embroidery anchors the circles against the linen.

Concentric Circles

by Alison Brookbanks

Finished size: 28 x 40 in/72 x 100 cm

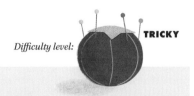

Difficulty level: **TRICKY**

MATERIALS

29 x 41 in/73.5 x 104 cm natural prewashed linen

Eight 12-x-27½-in/30.5-x-70-cm pieces coordinating printed fabrics

Sewing thread in coordinating colors

Two 6-in/15-cm square pieces, one linen and one coordinating print for the label

29 x 41 in/73.5 x 104 cm cotton fabric for backing

29 x 41 in/73.5 x 104 cm cotton batting

4 skeins cotton embroidery floss in coordinating colors

EXTRAS

Pencil

Alphabet stamps and fabric ink or permanent fabric pen

Compass

Embroidery needle

Safety pins

Disappearing fabric pen

TEMPLATE

Circle cutting pattern

TECHNIQUES

Piecing: concentric circles piecing

Hand stitches: running stitch or Sashiko embroidery, blind stitch or slip stitch

Quilting: Sashiko hand quilting

Binding: pillowcase method

NOTES

Seam allowances on outer quilt edges are ½ in/12 mm and circle seams are ¼ in/6 mm.

There are three concentric circle sets in this quilt and each is made in the same way. All instructions are the same for each circle series, and for the purposes of these instructions, circle #1 pieces are described and numbered.

DIFFICULTY

Because this quilt has so many pieces and they are assembled in a certain order, the project will require all of your attention. To get the Sashiko stitches even, you will need some practice, but luckily the quilt is finished simply with the pillowcase method.

CUTTING

Trace and cut out the pieces for the three circle sets. Keep in mind the following:

1. Use the template as your base for making the concentric circles pattern pieces.

2. The dotted line is the outside circumference for each circle; this stays the same for all the pattern pieces, unless othewise noted. Draw concentric circles for the inner circumference of the pattern pieces using a compass; these inner circles should gradually decrease in size for each subsequent ring.

3. You will need to draw ten concentric circle rings for the large circle, five for the medium circle, and four for the smallest circle. You will then transfer each of these pattern pieces onto separate pieces of

paper, and cut them out so that the outside circumference is the same and the inner circumference of the circles changes with each template—this forms the gradually decreasing size of the concentric circles.

4. Cut one pattern piece for the linen opening using the solid line on the outside of the circle template. You will need one for each circle series.

5. Cut one template for the outer piece for each circle series, using the dotted line as the outer circumference. Use this template to cut one piece for each circle of fabric series, and this is the piece that is sewn onto the hole you will cut out of your background fabric and to which the subsequent rings are attached.

6. Cut one center piece for each circle. This is made by using the outer circumference of each circle series as your template but not cutting any inner circumference—this remains a whole circle, since it forms the whole center piece.

7. Cut two of all the other rings in each series. Keeping them the same, use the dotted lines for the outer ring and the inner concentric circles you drew earlier for the inner circumference ring.

8. The ring templates for the concentric circles are made with the outer circumferences all the same and just the inner circumference gradually getting smaller. However, in the large circle series there is an optional change in the outer circumference about halfway down the pile, in order to save on fabric and make it less bulky.

9. Use a different fabric print for each ring in the series. Keep all the rings in each series together until you are ready to sew. You may find it helpful to cut them in order and keep them piled in order.

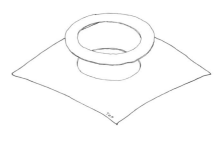

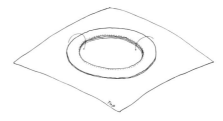

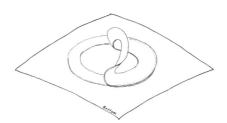

ASSEMBLING THE QUILT TOP

1. Arrange the linen circle-opening template pieces on the linen background and pin into place. Trace around the template with a pencil and then cut out the circles. This will make the holes in the quilt top in which the concentric circles will be sewn.

2. With the quilt top **Right**-side up, take piece #1, the largest ring shape, and pin to the linen opening. Sew around the edge and then clip into the seam allowance all the way around. Flip the ring through the opening so the raw edges are now hidden under the ring. Press the seam flat; the edge of the fabric ring will now be on the underside of the quilt top.

3. Turn the quilt top so that the underside is facing up. Take one of the next ring pieces and place it over the one you have just attached. With **Right** sides facing, pin outer edge to outer edge and sew the seam. You do not need to clip or press this open. It now forms the basis for the next ring to be attached.

4. Turn the quilt over again, with the quilt top facing **Right**-side up. Take the next ring piece, and, with **Right** sides facing, pin the inner circle openings together. Sew, clip, and turn under as before, then press neatly. Again, turn the quilt over with the underside facing up and attach the next ring piece with outer circumferences together.

5. Continue in this way until you reach the center. With the underside facing up, center the final piece, the smallest whole circle, over the opening. Pin in place to the last circle ring, and sew around the edge of the outer circumferences. Press.

6. Do the same for all the other circle series. When all three of the circle series have been made, press the entire front panel, making sure all the circles lay flat.

- -

MAKING THE TAG

1. Create an individual tag, by (1) stamping linen tape with fabric ink and alphabet stamps, (2) writing on it with permanent fabric pen, or (3) embroidering. Sew this between some linen and a strip of leftover print fabric, and trim the edges to form a perfect rectangle. Tuck the edges under and press flat. Next, pin in place on the backing piece of the quilt, and hand stitch around the edges.

- -

FINISHING THE QUILT

1. Lay the batting onto the back of the quilt top and baste into place with safety pins. Use a disappearing fabric pen to lightly draw a series of circles on the quilt top—trace circular objects with various circumferences, echoing the placement of circles on the quilt. Use embroidery floss to do a simple running stitch (or Sashiko embroidery, which consists of precisely measured running stitches—⅛ in/3 mm for the facing stitch, and 1⁄16 in/2 mm for the under stitch). Embroider each circle with a different color thread.

2. Place the backing fabric on top of the quilted top and batting, with **Right** sides together; pin edges of the quilt together and sew around the outside edge, leaving a 6-in/15-cm opening on one side. Clip the corners and turn **Right**-side out; press seams flat and neat. Hand sew the opening closed with a blind hem or slip stitch.

Geometric

Geometry, the science of relationships between objects, lines, and space, has provided designers and makers with a visual language for centuries. The designs in this section all deal in some way with the geometric principles of proportion, the relationships between objects and the patterns they make.

Shannon Lamden uses her senses to create a pleasing combination of fabrics in her simple Cheater's ("Aunty Cookie") Quilt; Lisa Call's Modern Geometric Quilt makes use of the principle of proportion to create a seemingly simple design; while Ruth Singer, in her Constellations Quilt, takes her inspiration from the relationships of the planets.

IN THIS SECTION: Cheater's ("Aunty Cookie") Quilt 120 ✻ Modern Geometric Quilt 124

Constellations Quilt 128 ✻ Windmill Quilt Project offered online at www.chroniclebooks.com/miniquilts

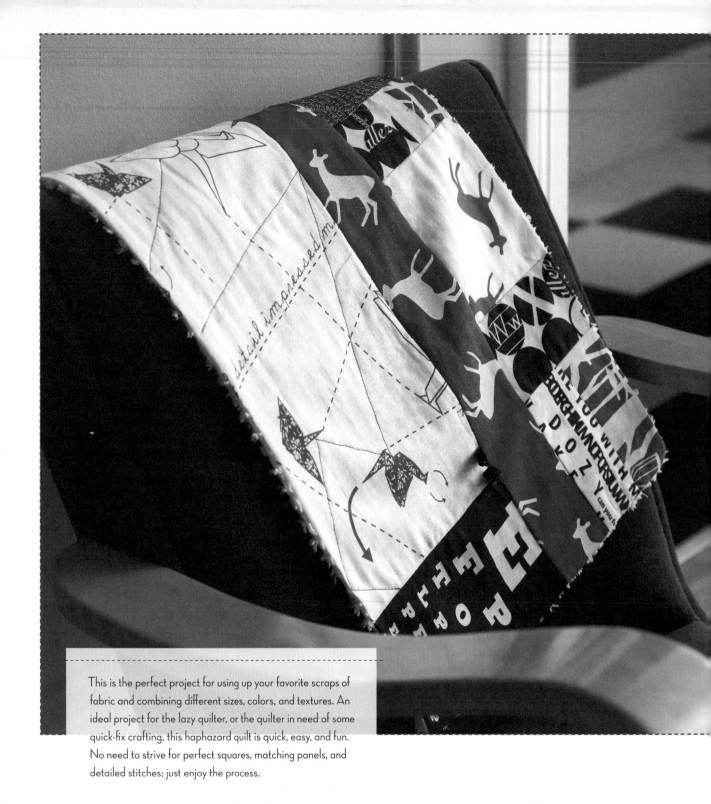

This is the perfect project for using up your favorite scraps of
fabric and combining different sizes, colors, and textures. An
ideal project for the lazy quilter, or the quilter in need of some
quick-fix crafting, this haphazard quilt is quick, easy, and fun.
No need to strive for perfect squares, matching panels, and
detailed stitches; just enjoy the process.

Cheater's ("Aunty Cookie") Quilt

by Shannon Lamden

Finished size: 22½ x 14½ in/57 x 37 cm

Difficulty level: **EASY**

MATERIALS

23 x 15 in/58.5 x 38 cm fabric for backing (ideally a textured fabric such as corduroy, terry cloth, chenille, or wool blanketing)

½ yd/46 cm total various fabrics for the quilt top

Cotton thread

Ribbon (optional)

EXTRA

Masking tape

TECHNIQUES

Piecing: improvisational piecing

Binding: pillowcase method

Quilting: optional machine quilting

NOTES

Seam allowances are all ¼ in/6 mm.

This project uses a basic palette—three or four colors at the most—with the backing fabric made of something textured, yet plain. The quilt top is made up from an assortment of fabrics in all different sizes, prints, and textures. The exact measurements are given here for this quilt, but feel free to improvise with your own quilt top.

The quilt top is put together first in three sections and then joined together to make a single large panel.

Attach some masking tape to your workbench to mark out the edges of the quilt. This saves you from having to remeasure throughout your design and planning process.

The backing is attached pillowcase-style; there is minimal quilting involved, and no batting. You can use batting if you wish, but if you use a heavy backing fabric then batting will not be needed.

When quilting, take your cue from the types of fabrics you have used. Some fabrics call for stripes or squares, while others require squiggles and circles. If you have used a lot of textured fabrics, then you may want to keep the quilting quite simple in order to avoid interfering with the texture of the fabrics.

DIFFICULTY

This is a super-simple quilt to make. It is all machine sewn, with no batting—perfect for a quick project or beginner quilter.

DESIGN

1. Measure the size of your finished quilt, this one being 22½ x 14½ in/57 x 37 cm, on your work space. Mark out the three sections with masking tape.

2. Lay out your fabric pieces. This is the fun part, where your own personal style comes into play. Your aim here is to fill the three sections with pieces of fabric that look good arranged together but still have that slightly ramshackle appearance. You will cut them to specific sizes next.

3. Fill section #1 with a larger piece and a smaller piece, section #2 with a long strip, and section #3 with an assortment of rectangles.

CUTTING

Cut one 23-x-15-in/58.5-x-38-cm piece of textured fabric for backing. Use your various quilt-top fabrics to cut out the following:

a. Cut one 18½-x-8-in/47-x-20-cm piece for section #1.

b. Cut one 4½-x-8-in/11.5-x-20-cm piece for section #1.

c. Cut one 23-x-3-in/58-x-7.5-cm piece for section #2.

d. Cut two 5½-x-2¾-in/14-x-7-cm pieces for section #3.

e. Cut two 3-x-2¾-in/7.5-x-7-cm pieces for section #3.

f. Cut one 4-x-5-in/10-x-12.5-cm piece for section #3.

g. Cut one 3½-x-5-in/9-x-12.5-cm piece for section #3.

h. Cut one 3¾-x-5-in/9.5-x-12.5-cm piece for section #3.

i. Cut one 5¾-x-5-in/14.5-x-12.5-cm piece for section #3.

- -

ASSEMBLING THE QUILT TOP

Once you are happy with the combination, pin and sew the small pieces in section #3 together, and press. Sew the two pieces in section #1 together, and press. Sew section #1 to section #2, and finally sew section #3 to section #2. Press the quilt top.

FINISHING

1. Attach the backing to the quilt top using the pillowcase finishing method described on page 41. Place the quilt top and backing **Right** sides together. Pin around the edges and sew, leaving a 4-in/10-cm opening for turning **Right**-side out. Use a chopstick to push the corners out. Press the quilt, making the edges even and neat, and sew up the opening either by machine or by hand, using a blind hemming stitch.

2. Hand sew or machine sew lines or a freestyle pattern through the quilt. If the fabric is quite textured then you may only want to tie a few knots here and there.

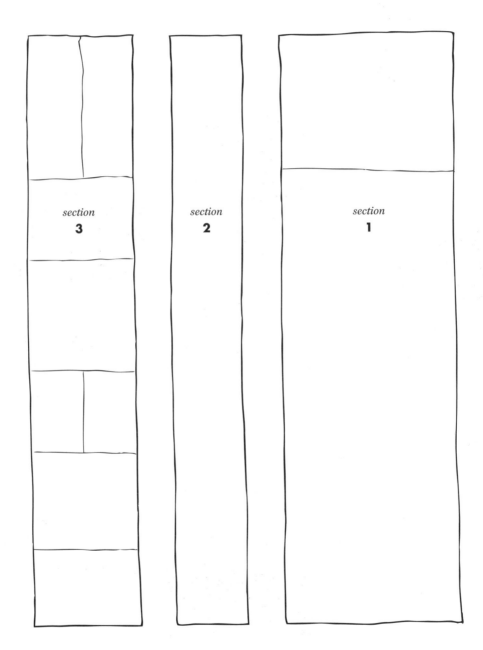

section
3

section
2

section
1

This quilt makes a bold statement, reminiscent of Mondrian's geometric abstract paintings. Using the principles of proportion in design, you can create a quilt that reflects your unique state of mind.

Modern Geometric Quilt

by Lisa Call

Finished size: 12 in/30.5 cm square

Difficulty level: **MEDIUM**

MATERIALS

- ½ yd/46 cm fabric in chosen main color for background, backing, binding, and hanging sleeve
- 4½ x 16 in/11 x 40.5 cm contrast fabric for lines
- 6-in/15-cm square fabric in accent color
- 14-in/35.5-cm square cotton batting
- Cotton quilting thread in coordinating colors

EXTRAS

- Design wall
- Tailor's chalk
- Rotary cutter, ruler, and cutting mat, or scissors
- Walking foot

TECHNIQUES

- Piecing: improvisational cutting and piecing
- Quilting: straight line machine quilting
- Binding: faced binding

NOTES

Seam allowances are all ¼ in/6 mm.

Hand-dyed fabrics are suggested but commercial solids will also work. Bold, solid colors are recommended. Prewash and iron all fabrics before cutting.

Press well after sewing each seam. Press seam allowances toward the background fabric.

A proportional design will allow the eye to move around without leaving the image—start with a strong focal point, and balance the spaces with opposing shapes. Set a very close stitch length and avoid crisscrossing your stitching.

Remember that you will lose a total of ½ in/12 mm for seam allowance in each of the shapes you create. Learning to compensate for the seam allowance in a design requires practice but makes improvisational piecing interesting.

It can be advantageous to place the background square on a design wall as you choose the location for the lines. (A design wall is simply a piece of felt or batting, attached to a wall, onto which fabric pieces will stick without the use of pins or tape.)

DIFFICULTY

This is the perfect quilt on which to practice improvisational cutting and piecing. It is finished with thin straight-line quilting and has a faced binding instead of a traditional binding.

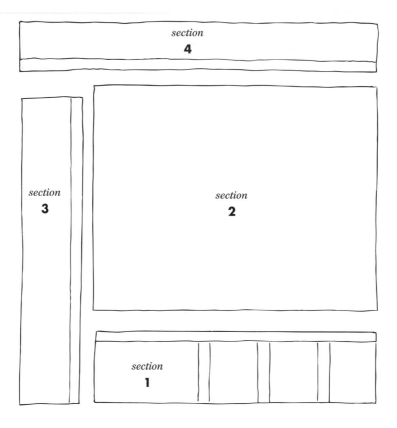

CUTTING AND DESIGN

1. Cut two 14-in/35.5-cm squares from the main color fabric for the background and backing.

2. Cut one ¼-in/6-mm length of 1½ yd/1.4 m from the main fabric for the faced binding.

3. Cut one 8-x-10½-in/20-x-26.5-cm piece from the main color fabric for the hanging sleeve.

4. Cut four 16-x-¾-in/40.5-x-2-cm strips from the contrast fabric for the lines.

5. Experiment with placing the contrast fabric strips in various spots on the background fabric until you are happy with the results, or you can use the placement shown in the diagram.

6. Step back from your design and look at it from a distance (a design wall comes in handy here). Then, as you finalize the placement for each of the lines, cut the strips of contrast fabric to the correct length for that section.

CUTTING YOUR BACKGROUND FABRIC

With tailor's chalk, mark where your lines are to be placed and move the strip of fabric out of the way. Cut the uppermost horizontal line first, the line on the left side second, the line at the bottom edge third, and the four rectangles last. Swap out one of the small rectangles at the bottom and replace with the accent piece (cut it to match the size of the piece you are replacing). You can use a rotary cutter, mat, and ruler, or scissors.

ASSEMBLING THE QUILT TOP

1. Sew the small rectangles and strips at the bottom section together first. Start with a rectangle and attach the strips and accent piece in the correct order. Press seams toward the background fabric. Then sew the strip to the top of the small rectangles; this forms section #1.

2. Attach section #2 to the top of section #1, remembering to press and trim with the rotary cutter as you go.

3. Sew a strip onto section #3 and another strip onto section #4, and press. Then attach section #3 to the side of the joined #1 and #2 sections. Finally, attach section #4 to the top.

4. Trim the quilt top to 12½ in/32 cm square. Don't forget to think about proportion when trimming the edges of your piece. Press the entire piece flat with a steam iron.

FINISHING THE QUILT

1. Make a quilt sandwich with the quilt top, batting, and backing and baste together using your preferred basting method.

2. Using the walking foot on your sewing machine, and cotton thread in coordinating colors, quilt in parallel lines that are approximately ⅛ in/3 mm apart. Quilt all of one color background before changing the thread color to quilt the different color sections.

3. Attach a hanging sleeve to the back using the instructions on page 45. Attach a faced binding (see page 42). Using a facing rather than traditional binding gives this quilt its clean, modern appearance.

This quilt is a simple geometric design using reverse appliqué techniques; it is inspired by and named for the striking patterns that stars and planets make in the night sky.

Constellations Quilt

by Ruth Singer

Finished size: 20 in/50 cm square

Difficulty level: **MEDIUM**

MATERIALS

⅝ yd/57 cm fine wale corduroy, to contrast with wool felt

¼ yd/23 cm coordinating fabric for binding

20-in/50-cm square wool felt

Pack of transparent or pearlescent sequins

Thread in color to match wool felt

20-in/50-cm square cotton quilt batting

Embroidery floss

EXTRAS

Paper

Fabric marking pen, pencil, or tailor's chalk

Small, sharp scissors

Leather punch

Thimble

Disappearing-ink pen (optional)

Pressing cloth

TECHNIQUES

Appliqué: reverse raw edge appliqué

Quilting: hand quilting

Hand stitch: running stitch

Binding: mitered corner binding

TEMPLATE

Quilt top design

NOTES

Seam allowances are all ¼ in/6 mm.

You can use the suggested placement of circles or create your own arrangement.

The layers of heavy fabric (corduroy and felt) can make this quilt hard to sew by hand; using a thimble is an enormous help, or you can try using a lighter-weight fabric.

DIFFICULTY

This is not a difficult quilt—it incorporates simple sewing, minimal quilting, and basic traditional binding. However, because the fabric is quite heavy, the hand quilting will be difficult. There are some interesting techniques here to experiment with, including using a leather punch on your felt to help create designs and reverse appliqué.

CUTTING

1. Cut two 20-in/50-cm squares from the corduroy fabric—one for the background and one for the quilt back.

2. Cut two 2-in/5-cm strips from the binding fabric. You will want to end up with approximately 2½ yd/2.3 m of binding.

CREATING YOUR DESIGN

1. Trace and cut circle shapes onto paper, using any circular objects such as jars, bottles, and cups you may have around the house.

2. Place the piece of wool felt facedown and scatter your paper circles on it, making sure none are too close to the edge. Draw around them with a fabric-marking pen, pencil, or chalk.

3. Cut out the circles from the felt. Use a small pair of sharp scissors to make a cut in the center of the circle, and then carefully cut around the drawn outline. Repeat for all circles.

4. Make the small dots surrounding the smaller circles. First, mark the positions with chalk or pen, following the pattern, or as desired. Use a sharp leather punch to stamp the holes. If your leather punch has variable sizes, then try different sizes for different circles.

5. Sew the sequins around a couple of the larger holes, using a thread that blends in with the wool felt. Sew the sequins on one at a time, by bringing the thread up through the center hole, then stitching to the left side. Bring the needle through to the opposite side of the sequin and then down through the center hole. Continue to the next sequin, using the same thread.

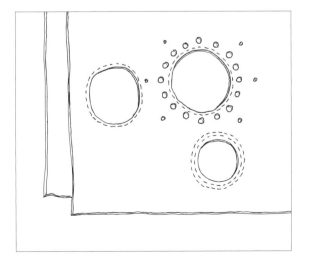

ASSEMBLING THE QUILT

1. Make a quilt sandwich with one piece of corduroy for the backing, facedown, on the bottom, and then add the batting, followed by another layer of corduroy, face up, and the wool felt faceup on the very top. Pin and baste in place.

2. Hand quilt through all the layers using a running stitch and the embroidery floss. Sew in concentric circles around the holes in the felt, starting with a row closest to the cut edges of the felt holes, to hold everything together.

3. To hide the thread ends, knot the thread, then pass the needle under the hole to fasten in the wool felt layer only. You can mark the stitching lines first if you wish, using a disappearing-ink pen. Either follow the illustration or experiment with the number of circles you use on your quilt. You may wish to vary the stitch length on the quilting stitch to add interest.

FINISHING THE QUILT

1. When all the stitching is complete, lightly press the quilt top with an iron set for hot steam and a pressing cloth to avoid damaging the wool felt or the sequins.

2. Bind the edges of the quilt using your preferred method. A straight-grain single-fold binding is used here (see page 39), with the same corduroy used in the background and backing.

Punk, Pop, and Politics

Political crafting has a long history. Incorporating subversive political messages in their quilts was one of the ways early American women could express their political views. Today, political crafting is still going strong—sometimes outrageous, sometimes subversive. Pop art and punk craft is a more recent phenomenon that reflects the attitudes of the current generation.

Nicole Vaughan's homage to her nanna, Granny's Delight, is a tongue-in-cheek design; Liz Harvatine's 1984 ("Pegasus Rainbow") Quilt takes its inspiration from the kitschy and corny 1980s; Lisa Solomon's double-sided Target Pillow is playful, with a subtle message; while Boo Davis's diptych, Two Heads Are Better than One, uses a traditional step block to create a punk-inspired design.

IN THIS SECTION: *Granny's Delight* 132 * *1984 ("Pegasus Rainbow") Quilt* 136

Target Pillow 142 * *Two Heads Are Better than One* 146

This mini quilt explores childhood memories of "Nanna"—of toast and tea served on mismatched china, of false teeth and handmade doilies on the dresser. This quilt is a cheeky homage to grandmothers everywhere. It is designed for you to create your own version with different design elements—teacup, false teeth, and granny silhouette—to embroider or stencil. It's a perfect project for personalizing, so feel free to make your own templates that reflect your memories of your grandmother.

Granny's Delight

by Nicole Vaughan

Finished size: yellow quilt 13 x 17 in/33 x 43 cm; brown and pink quilt 14 x 18 in/35.5 x 46 cm

Difficulty level: **EASY**

MATERIALS

⅓ yd/30.5 cm patterned quilting cotton fabric

⅓ yd/30.5 cm solid quilting cotton fabric

½ yd/46 cm muslin for backing and binding, either tea-stained or unbleached

16 x 20 in/40.5 x 50 cm 100 percent cotton quilt batting

16 in/40.5 cm mini rickrack braid in complementary color

Embroidery floss, or thread, in contrasting color

1 or 2 skeins white and tea-stained, or variegated beige, embroidery floss

Doily, either vintage or new

Accent button

EXTRAS

Rotary cutter, transparent ruler, and cutting mat

Iron-on transfer pencil or carbon paper

Embroidery needle

Freezer paper, craft knife, fabric paint, and sponge brush for stenciling (optional)

Hand-quilting needle

Thimble

Chalk or embroidery transfer pen

TEMPLATES

Teacup

Granny silhouette

False teeth

List continues next page

NOTES

Seam allowances are all ¼ in/6 mm.

Use the photograph as a guide for placing the design elements—or place them as you like!

Dye the doily, the binding fabric, and embroidery floss using the tea-dye instructions on page 27 if you want that vintage look.

Decide which method you will use for the design elements—stenciling or embroidery or both. If you choose stenciling, see page 26 for stenciling instructions. If you are embroidering, use 3 strands of embroidery floss.

Instructions are given for finishing this quilt in two different ways, however the materials list is just for making one quilt.

DIFFICULTY

This quilt is nice and easy. It requires simple piecing of the quilt background, along with just enough embroidery to add a little bit of a challenge. The quilt also requires some screen printing or stenciling. How much hand quilting you do and the type of binding you choose will depend on your level of skill and enthusiasm.

CUTTING

1. For the yellow quilt:

   a. Cut one 13½-x-7½-in/34-x-19-cm piece of patterned fabric.

   b. Cut one 13½-x-10½-in/34-x-26.5-cm piece of solid fabric.

c. Cut one 15-x-20-in/38-x-50-cm piece of backing fabric.

d. Cut one 15-x-20-in/38-x-50-cm piece of batting.

For the brown and pink quilt:

a. Cut one 14½-x-10-in/37-x-25-cm piece of patterned fabric.

b. Cut one 14½-x-9-in/37-x-23-cm piece of solid fabric.

c. Cut one 16-x-20-in/40.5-x-50-cm piece of backing fabric.

d. Cut one 16-x-20-in/40.5-x-50-cm piece of batting.

2. Cut 2-in/5-cm strips of the binding fabric to make approximately 2½ yd/2.3 m of double-fold binding.

Continued from page 133

TECHNIQUES

Decorative elements: tea dyeing and stenciling

Hand stitches: backstitch, chain stitch or stem stitch, running stitch, split stitch, French knots, and whipstitch or blanket stitch

Binding: pillowcase method or mitered corner binding

ASSEMBLING THE QUILT TOP

1. With **Right** sides together, sew the two pieces of fabric for the quilt top together with your sewing machine, and press seams open. Machine or hand sew the mini rickrack braid over the seam you've just sewn.

2. If you are embroidering your motif design elements, trace your teacup, granny, and false teeth motifs from the templates onto the quilt top. You could use an iron-on transfer pencil or carbon paper to do this. Embroider around the perimeter of the designs with the embroidery needle using an outline stitch of your choice, such as backstitch, chain stitch, or stem stitch.

Alternatively, if you are stenciling any of the motifs, then trace the template with freezer paper, cut out the design carefully using a craft knife and iron the design in place. Once the stencil is in place, sponge your fabric paint over the stencil, using thin layers and waiting for them to dry in between, until you have a result you are pleased with. You may need to set the fabric paint with an iron—please be sure to read the manufacturer's instructions first.

3. At this point, decide whether you will do a pillowcase binding or a traditional binding.

If you are using the pillowcase finishing method, as on the yellow quilt, follow the instructions on page 41. Once you are finished, hand sew a simple running stitch in a contrasting thread or embroidery floss color around the perimeter of the quilt.

If you are using a traditional binding, as on the brown and pink quilt, assemble a quilt sandwich (backing facedown, batting and quilt top faceup) and safety-pin baste the layers together. The binding will go on at the very last step.

FINISHING THE QUILT

1. For either quilt, the next step is to add any additional hand quilting or embroidery and embellishments.

2. Using the tea-stained or beige floss, embellish the patterned fabric with running stitches, split stitches, French knots—whatever suits the pattern on the fabric.

3. Pin the doily to a corner of the solid fabric, and attach it to your quilt with a whipstitch or blanket stitch around the edge to hold it in place. Sew on your button.

4. At this point, if you used the pillowcase finishing method, press with an iron set for hot steam, and you're done.

5. If you chose to do a traditional binding, then you still need to attach the binding. Follow the double-fold mitered corner binding instructions on page 41. Press and you are done.

This quilt is inspired by the 1980s, with its pastels and kitschy accessories. Have fun with this quilt. Feel free to go crazy with color and use your own cute stencil.

1984 ("Pegasus Rainbow") Quilt

by Liz Harvatine

Finished size: 16 x 22 in/40.5 x 56 cm

Difficulty level: **EASY**

MATERIALS

½ yd/46 cm pink quilting cotton

18 x 22 in/46 x 56 cm various bright-colored or pastel quilting cottons (here, I have used blue, teal, yellow polka-dotted, light blue polka-dotted, and green cottons)

⅓ yd/30.5 cm white quilting cotton

White cotton thread

17 x 23 in/43 x 58.5 cm thin cotton batting

EXTRAS

Transparent ruler, rotary cutter, and cutting mat

Masking tape

Disappearing-ink pen

Freezer paper

Craft knife

White fabric paint (or screen-printing ink)

Sponge brush

Walking foot

TEMPLATE

Pegasus

TECHNIQUES

Decorative element: stenciling

Binding: pillowcase method

Hand stitch: slip stitch

Quilting: machine quilting

NOTES

Seam allowances on outer quilt edges are ½ in/12 mm and all other seams are ¼ in/6 mm.

A disappearing-ink fabric pen is used in this project to allow you to draw on both sides of the fabric without worrying about marks. The ink will fade after a couple of days or will come out with a tiny dab of water. If you want to use something else to mark the quilt, be sure that you have a way to remove the mark. If that means washing the whole quilt, prewash your fabrics!

DIFFICULTY

This quilt has some unique piecing, which means you have to pay attention to cutting and measuring; however, once you have this taken care of, the quilt goes together very easily. With only minimal quilting, it's a snap. There is some freezer stenciling involved, which is fun. If you haven't done this before, try a practice run on some scrap fabric before stenciling right on your finished quilt top.

CUTTING

1. Cut the quilt top pieces using a ruler, rotary cutter, and cutting mat. Cut one piece from each of the colored quilt top fabrics (feel free to substitute you own fabric selections) according to the following measurements:

    a. Cut one 2-x-12-in/5-x-30.5-cm piece pink fabric.

    b. Cut one 4-x-13-in/10-x-33-cm piece blue fabric.

    c. Cut one 5-x-12-in/12.5-x-30.5-cm piece teal fabric.

d. Cut one 8-x-10-in/20-x-25-cm piece yellow fabric.

e. Cut one 7-x-10½-in/17-x-26.5-cm piece light blue fabric.

f. Cut one 9-x-11-in/23-x-28-cm piece green fabric.

g. Cut two 5-in/12.5-cm strips of white fabric, along the entire cross grain of the fabric. Fold these in half, matching the short ends. Cutting through both layers, cut two white pieces to correspond with the widths of your six colored fabrics. You should end up with:

i. two 2-in/5-cm pieces

ii. two 4-in/10-cm pieces

iii. two 5-in/12.5-cm pieces

iv. two 8-in/20-cm pieces

v. two 7-in/17-cm pieces

vi. two 9-in/23-cm pieces

2. Cut one 17-x-23-in/43-x-58.5-cm piece from the pink fabric for the backing.

- -

DESIGNING THE QUILT TOP

1. Sew the corresponding widths of the white fabric onto both ends of the colored strips of fabric.

2. Using a ruler, rotary cutter, and cutting mat, cut all strips, except for the pink, into thinner strips. Cut a variety of widths, no smaller than 1¼ in/3 cm and no wider than 2½ in/6 cm.

3. On your work table, lay two 35-in/90-cm strips of masking tape, parallel to each other and 17 in/43 cm apart. On the top strip of tape, make a mark 4 in/10 cm in from the left.

4. Take one of the fabric strips and lay it down over the tape so that the bottom left edge lines up with the end of the bottom strip of tape and the top left edge lines up with the mark you made on the top strip. The white fabric on either end must extend beyond both strips of tape, with the colored fabric placed somewhere in the middle.

5. Lay out the rest of your fabric strips beside the first, carefully lining them up at the same angle. The colored fabric does not need to be perfectly centered between the tape lines—just be sure the white extends over the inner edge of the tape at both ends. If you want to be extra safe, you can tape down the ends of each piece as you go to make sure they stay in place.

6. Check to make sure that the colors look good together. Strips of the same color should not be placed next to each other, but they shouldn't form a pattern (it's meant to be a little random). Begin and end with different colors.

7. Lay a transparent ruler over your strips along the upper tape line, being careful not to move the strips. Use a disappearing-ink pen to draw along the edge of the ruler across all of the strips, gently lifting and moving the ruler over if it is not long enough.

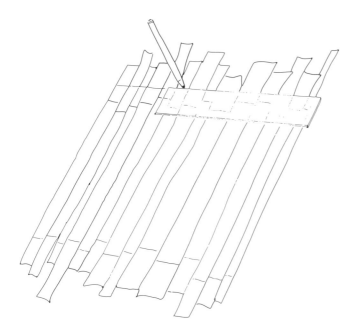

8. Now, stack your strips in the order in which you've laid them out, with the left-most strip on the top and the right-most on the bottom. (You might like to number them above the marked line; this part will be trimmed off later.)

ASSEMBLING THE QUILT TOP

1. To sew the strips together, start with the left-most strip. Lay it in front of you, **Right**-side up; the end without the line should be closest to you. Lay the next strip on top, **Right**-side down, with right edges matching. Adjust the top strip so that the two disappearing-ink lines intersect ¼ in/6 mm in from the edge, where the seam line will be. Do not match up the lines at the edge. Use a ruler if you need to. You should be able to see the ink through the white fabric. If not, stick a pin through the top piece at the correct point, then through the bottom piece, and bring them together. When the two strips

are properly aligned, sew them together with a ¼-in/6-mm seam. When you open up the pieces you will have a straight line across both.

2. Open up the first two pieces and then place the next strip, **Right** side facing down, onto the right edge, and sew in the same manner described above. Continue until all of the strips are pieced. Press all seams open; do not press to the side, since this creates more bulk and you need the quilt top to be as flat as possible when you stencil.

3. Square off the left side of the quilt ½ in/12 mm in from the end of the line at the top left corner, cutting perpendicular to the line. Sew this piece onto the right-hand side of the quilt, matching the disappearing-ink line the way you did when sewing the pieces together and making the quilt top into a rectangle shape.

4. Square up the finished quilt top. Using a ruler, rotary cutter and cutting mat, cut along the line at the top of the quilt. Trim the bottom edge so that the quilt top is 17 in/43 cm high. Carefully line up the quilt on your cutting mat to make sure that your cuts are parallel. Square off the sides of the quilt top so that it is 23 in/58.5 cm wide.

STENCILING

1. Trace the Pegasus motif onto the matte side of a piece of freezer paper. The paper should extend at least 3 in/7.5 cm beyond the edge of the graphic. With a craft knife, carefully cut the shape out of the paper, keeping the edges intact. Then, with a dry iron set on high heat, press the freezer paper stencil into position onto the quilt top. Be sure to press down all inner edges of the stencil.

2. Load a little bit of fabric paint onto your sponge brush and dab the brush up and down inside the stencil. Do not brush side to side, because this might cause you to push paint under the edges. Fill the shape with a thin layer of paint and let dry (you can use a hair dryer to speed this up). If you need more paint, add another thin layer. Continue until the paint is sufficiently opaque. When the paint is totally dry, carefully pull off the stencil and heat set the paint according to the instructions; this usually means ironing it or putting it in the dryer on a hot setting.

FINISHING THE QUILT

1. Make a quilt sandwich, according to the pillowcase method. Align all edges and pin the quilt top, batting, and backing together. Sew with the pillowcase finishing method (see page 41). Sew ½ in/ 12 mm in from the raw edge through all three layers, around the entire quilt, leaving a 7-in/17-cm opening at the bottom. Trim the corners.

2. Turn the quilt **Right**-side out through the opening and push out the corners. Press, turning in the edges of the opening, and slip stitch the opening closed by hand.

3. Baste the layers either by hand or with safety pins. With a walking foot on your sewing machine, quilt just to the right of each diagonal seam all the way from top to bottom.

4. Finish the quilt off with a name tag and a hanging sleeve on the back (see page 45).

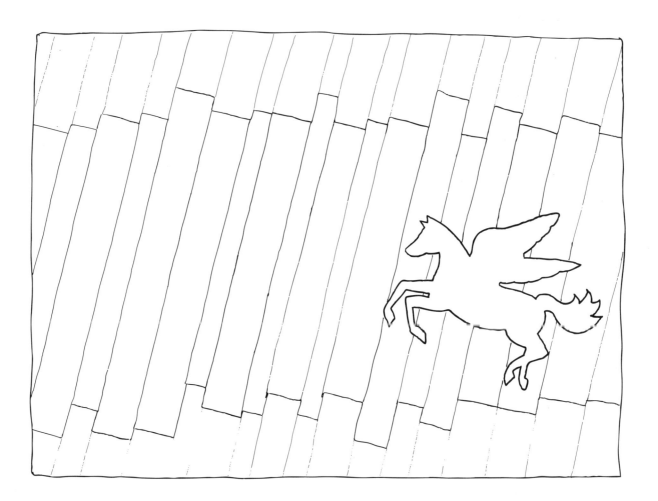

The inspiration for this pillow comes from vintage rifle targets
and plays with the interpretation of gender and domesticity.
This quilt is actually a double-sided pillow, with one side mimick-
ing the more traditional rifle target and the other side a visual
play on color and pattern. Choose any colors you like here and
mix and match to your heart's content.

Target Pillow

by Lisa Solomon

Finished size: 18 in/46 cm square

Difficulty level: **MEDIUM**

MATERIALS

⅝ yd/57 cm medium-weight cotton duck

¼ yd/23 cm black wool felt for black targets

4 or 5 (at least 8-x-10-in/20-x-25-cm) pieces of coord-inating fabrics for colorful targets (each 8-x-10-in/20-x-25-cm piece of fabric makes one set of targets)

One 6-in/15-cm square cotton fabric for bunny #1

Two 6-in/15-cm squares wool felt for bunny #2

Crochet cord or embroidery floss in a light neutral color, such as cream

Cotton thread in colors that coordinate with the circles, including black

16-in/40.5-cm zipper

18-in/46-cm square pillow form, or enough stuffing to stuff a pillow that size

EXTRAS

Cardboard or heavy card stock to make target templates

Fabric glue

Quilting ruler

Fray-check spray

Zipper foot

TEMPLATES

Bunny

List continues next page

NOTES

The pillow is constructed from medium-weight cotton duck canvas, but a lighter cotton or linen can be substituted, if you like.

The black targets are made of wool felt, due to its tendency not to fray.

For the colorful targets and one of the rabbit silhouettes, use patterned fabrics.

Because of the wool felt and the raw edges of the cotton target circles, the finished quilt is best washed by hand.

If you wish to make only one side of this pillow and use it as a quilt for hanging on a wall, you can put it together with the backing, using the simple pillowcase finishing method described on page 41.

Thank you to Lara Cameron (laracameron.com) for the fabric used on the bright side of this pillow.

DIFFICULTY

Cutting the circles and hand stitching around the black felt target takes the most time. Sewing in the zipper is the most difficult part, since there is no quilting involved.

CUTTING

1. Trace and cut out the bunny template from cardboard or card stock, and use cups to trace four circles with the largest circle 5-in/12.7-cm in diameter, and the smallest 1-in/2.5-cm.

2. Cut two 20-in/50-cm squares from the cotton duck fabric.

3. Cut four sets of the target circle template (each set is made up of five different-sized circles) from the black felt.

4. Cut four or five sets of the target circle template from the various coordinating fabrics.

5. Cut one bunny from the cotton fabric.

6. Cut two bunnies from the felt.

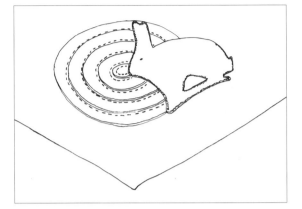

ASSEMBLING THE BLACK TARGET SIDE

1. Lay all the felt 5-in/12.5-cm circles on a flat surface and glue all the 4-in/10-cm circles on the centers (you can use a ruler for accuracy). Then, using the crochet cord or embroidery floss, back-stitch around the 4-in/10-cm circle.

2. Repeat with all five layers of circles, gluing and stitching together the same way.

3. Fold one of your 20-in/50-cm squares of cotton duck into quarters and use a hot iron to press the

Continued from page 143

TECHNIQUES

Hand stitches: backstitch, straight stitch

Appliqué: machine appliqué

Binding: pillowcase method

Other: Inserting a zipper

edges; this will give you guidelines to follow. With your ruler, find the center of each quadrant and pin your four targets securely in place. With black thread, machine stitch around the outer edge of each target and then also around the outer edge of the 2-in/5-cm circle.

4. Place the cotton-fabric bunny, **Right**-side up, on top of one of the felt bunnies, and pin them together. Using a zigzag stitch on your sewing machine, sew them together around the outer edges. Then pin in place on your target (lower right-hand corner) and sew, with your machine, around the perimeter of the bunny using a straight stitch.

MAKING THE PATTERNED TARGET SIDE

1. Take your patterned circle pieces and mix and match your fabric circles until you have four stacks you are happy with. Use fray-check spray along the edges if you need to, or use a zigzag stitch around the outer edges of the circles (using color-coordinated thread).

2. Pin the 4-in/10-cm circles onto the center of the 5-in/12.5-cm circles and straight stitch them together. Repeat with the remaining circles until all five layers are sewn into place.

3. Fold the second 20-in/50-cm square of cotton duck into quarters and use a hot iron to press the edges; this will give you guidelines to follow. With your ruler, find the center of each quadrant and pin the four targets securely in place. With coordinating thread, machine stitch around the outer edge of each target and then also around the outer edge of the inner circle.

4. Place and pin your felt bunny onto the lower-left target (facing the opposite direction if you like). Use fabric glue to attach the bunny, and, when dry, straight stitch around the edge.

FINISHING THE PILLOW

1. Before you sew the two sides together, you need to put your zipper in. Place the **Right** sides of the pillow squares together and pin, and then sew a 1-in/2.5-cm basting seam along one side of the pillow only. Lay flat and press the seam open.

2. Then lay your zipper down along the seam line, with the **Right** side of the zipper positioned so it is facing the **Wrong** side of the seam. Make sure the zipper is lying exactly centered along the seam line. Pin into place.

3. Using the zipper foot on your machine, sew along each side of the zipper. Then unpick the basted seam you sewed earlier and your zipper is now in place.

4. With the zipper at least halfway unzipped, place the **Right** sides of the pillow together and sew the other three sides of the pillow with a 1-in/2.5-cm seam allowance. You can trim the seam allowance down a little and clip the corners to get rid of some of the bulk. You may also want to zigzag the raw edges to keep them from fraying. Turn the pillow **Right**-side out and press.

5. Fill with a pillow form and display on your couch.

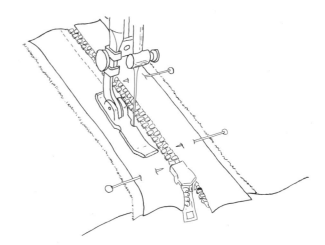

Contemplate balance, harmony, and mortality with your very own patchwork *memento mori*. Here, a traditional winding stairway block design collides with a pair of skulls in a lively diptych. At 392 pieces, this template-free project is a crash course in rotary cutting and chain sewing. No use for soothing colors and pretty fabrics here—the more garish and ugly, the better!

Two Heads Are Better than One

by Boo Davis

Finished size: 20½ x 19 in/52 x 48 cm (each panel of the diptych)

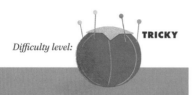

Difficulty level: **TRICKY**

MATERIALS

½ yd/46 cm each colors 1 and 2 quilting fabrics (gray and white)

¼ yd/23 cm each colors 3 through 6 quilting fabrics (black, brown, orange, and pink)

1⅓ yds/1.2 m quilting fabric for backing and binding

Cotton thread

Two 24½-x-23-in/62-x-58.5-cm pieces cotton batting

EXTRAS

Rotary cutter, ruler, and cutting mat

TECHNIQUES

Piecing: chain piecing

Quilting: machine straight-line quilting

Binding: mitered corner binding

NOTES

Seam allowances are all ¼ in/6 mm.

Prewash fabrics if you are making pillows instead of the diptych, or something that will require washing later.

The quilts are constructed out of four blocks that are joined to make a rectangle of 20½ x 19 in/52 x 48 cm.

Mix in a few prints with the solids to create haphazard charm.

There are 392 total pieces in two different sizes. (See chart on page 148.)

The cutting and materials specifications here are enough to make the pair of quilts.

DIFFICULTY

This mini quilt diptych, though not difficult, is time consuming (it will take 16 to 20 hours) and requires precise cutting and organization of your squares. Once you begin chain sewing the pieces together, you will get it done in no time. If you are new to chain sewing, read the techniques on page 23. The key to success with this project is to keep your pieces well organized and press between each batch.

CUTTING

1. The following sizes include a ¼-in/6-mm seam allowance. You will be cutting pieces in two different sizes: rectangle #1 = 1½ x 2½ in/ 4 x 6 cm, and square #2 = 1½ x 1 ½ in/4 x 4 cm.

2. Color 1 (gray): Cut 82 of #1 and 10 of #2.

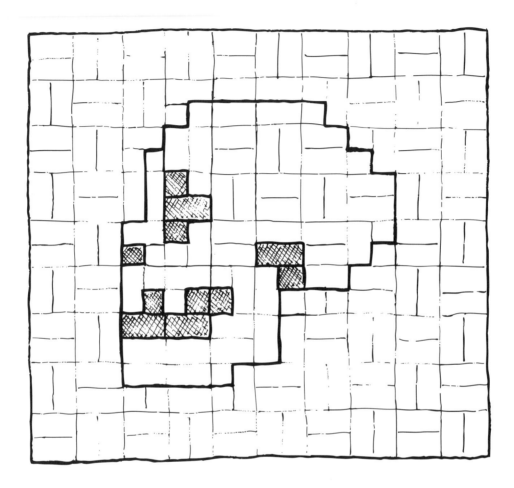

3. Color 2 (white): Cut 78 of #1 and 24 of #2.

4. Color 3 (black): Cut 48 of #1 and 16 of #2.

5. Color 4 (brown): Cut 44 of #1.

6. Color 5 (orange): Cut 42 of #1 and 2 of #2.

7. Color 6 (pink): Cut 34 of #1 and 12 of #2.

8. Here is how to accomplish these cutting tasks:

   a. Starting with your first color and continuing with all the subsequent colors, fold each large piece of fabric in half on a cutting mat from selvage to selvage. Align the folded edge along a grid line near the bottom of your cutting mat. Using the grid on your cutting mat, position a ruler and use a rotary cutter to trim off the cut edge of the fabric. Discard the edge.

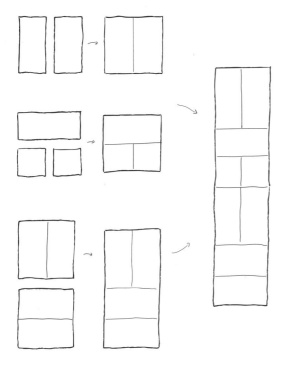

b. Measure a 2⅜-in/6-cm strip, selvage to selvage, and cut. Measure another 2⅜-in/6-cm strip and cut. Carefully position these strips directly on top of each other. Rotate them so they are horizontal along the cutting mat and align with the grid.

c. Trim off selvage at the ends and discard. Measure a 1½-in/4-cm piece and cut, continue to cut 1½-x-2⅜-in/4-x-6-cm rectangles. With remaining fabric, cut into 1½-in/4-cm squares.

d. Cut until you have enough pieces for each color. Arrange your rectangles and squares next to your sewing machine along with the diagram in their color-coded piles.

e. Cut two 24½-x-23-in/62-x-58.5-cm pieces of fabric for backing.

f. Cut enough 2-in/5-cm strips for binding so that you end up with a continuous strip that is 4½ yd/4.1 m long. Follow the pressing instructions for single-fold binding on page 39.

- -

CHAIN SEWING THE PIECES

1. As mentioned in the Notes section, on page 147, this quilt is made up of four blocks or quarters; see the diagram dividing the quilt this way. You will be making each block separately. Starting with the top-left block, locate all of the 1½-in/4-cm squares and sew each to the adjacent square. Press the seams toward the darker fabric and set aside (see the diagram that locates all the smaller squares).

2. Organize your rectangles into pairs, using the chart as a guide. Then, starting with the upper-left corner, take the first pair of rectangles of fabric and sew together into a square. Sew the rectangles together in a chain to save time and thread. Working

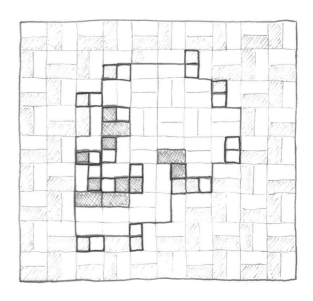

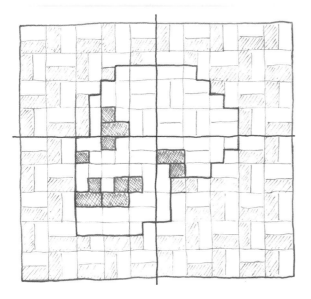

from left to right, according to the quilt diagram, grab the next two rectangles that form that square. Continue to sew the pairs of rectangles, moving in order from left to right and top to bottom.

3. Now that you have a continuous thread of sewn pairs, lay the still-attached pairs of rectangles on your ironing board. Use scissors to cut apart the threads. Press each seam toward the darker fabric.

- -

ASSEMBLING THE QUILT TOP

1. Arrange the pieces as they appear in the diagram for block #1 (all the rectangles should now be sewn into squares). Sew the top-left square to the square directly below it, and then attach the next square in that row, and continue until all the squares are sewn into their respective rows. Press the seams to one side.

2. Now it's time to sew the rows together. Face **Right** sides together and secure with pins. Remove the pins as you sew. Continue until you have finished one quarter and press the seams all to one side. Repeat on the remaining three blocks (quarters), and then sew the four blocks together. Repeat these steps for the second half of the diptych (the other quilt in the pair). This time you will make a mirror image—use a mirror, if necessary.

- -

FINISHING THE QUILT

1. Finish with quilting and binding the pair of quilts (see page 41). These pieces have been quilted using simple edge-to-edge diagonal lines. The quilts can be framed and hung on a wall, applied to a pair of pillows, or simply displayed wherever you'd like a reminder to carpe diem!

Memories and Storytelling

Memory and storytelling quilts are both important aspects of quilting tradition. They help us to preserve our past by using bits of old and treasured fabrics together with imagery that triggers our memories. These quilts can be made to commemorate a special occasion, offering a wonderful bonding or healing experience.

The Keepsake Quilt by Sherri-Lynn Wood has been made from the sentimental clothing remnants of mother and baby to celebrate the early years of the baby's life, while Jude Hill's Imagine is a fairy-tale quilt based on a single word and containing wonderful characters, interesting fabrics, and textures.

IN THIS SECTION:

Keepsake Quilt 152

Imagine 156

Many parents tuck away special pieces of their children's clothing as keepsakes. This mini quilt combines one such piece of clothing with the mother's favorite maternity outfit to commemorate the symbiotic, nurturing relationship between mother and child. Much like parenting, the design process is improvisational and full of challenge, discovery, and delight.

Keepsake Quilt

by Sherri-Lynn Wood

Finished size: depends on your preference and garments used

Difficulty level:  **TRICKY**

MATERIALS

A special piece of clothing saved from the child's early years

Mother's favorite maternity outfit

1 yd/91 cm cotton batting (depending on size of quilt)

1 yd/91 cm material for backing, a baby blanket, or other special fabric (depending on size of quilt)

Cotton quilting thread in contrasting or coordinating colors

EXTRAS

Tailor's chalk

Rotary cutter, ruler, and cutting mat

Fray-check spray

TECHNIQUES

Piecing: improvisational piecing and curved piecing

Appliqué: simple hand-stitched appliqué

Hand stitches: running stitch and slip stitch or blanket stitch

Quilting: hand quilting

Binding: mitered corner binding

NOTES

Seam allowances are all ¼ in/6 mm.

This project is more a recipe for how to create your own keepsake quilt than a step-by-step tutorial on how to re-create this one. However, if you do wish to re-create this quilt, you will need an adult's long-sleeved, collared cotton shirt and a two-piece toddler outfit also made from cotton.

The fabrics used in this quilt are cotton shirting materials; if you wish to use stretch fabrics you will need to stabilize the fabric by spraying with a heavy-duty starch or using fusible interfacing. Alternatively, you can iron on freezer paper, to stabilize the fabric while piecing, which can then be removed later. You may also need to use fray-check spray to control unraveling edges.

If you are using any delicate or see-through fabrics such as lace, you may have to line them first with plain cotton before piecing them into your quilt top. Add saved buttons, jewelry, or other mementos for embellishments.

DIFFICULTY

The amount of improvisational piecing in this quilt makes it a tricky project. You will need to have some confidence in your skills, or at least be methodical in your approach. If you have not sewn in this way before, then use this quilt as a learning experience in experimentation and improvisation.

CUTTING

1. Cut along the seam lines of the clothing to deconstruct the piece: cut the arms out along the shoulder seams, the sleeves along the arm seams, the body along the side seams, and so on. Preserve the features you want to highlight, such as the collar area, the front section with buttons or motifs, pockets, and cuffs.

2. Once you have deconstructed the clothing into sections, cut out the seams, hems, and linings to reduce any bulk. There is no need to pick out the seams; instead, cut along either side of the seam and discard the seam section.

ASSEMBLING THE PIECE

1. To make the "heart" of the quilt, begin with a piece of infant clothing. Choose a part of the clothing that has some interesting detail. Here, the baby's shirt has a boat motif on the front. This has been kept intact, with the collar and part of the shoulder still attached.

2. You will now use fabric from the mother's shirt to complete the quilt block that forms the center of the quilt. Use sections from the back of the mother's

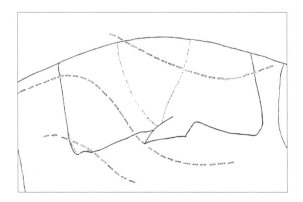

shirt to form a background on which to appliqué the baby's shirt front and collar. If you have curved pieces from the shoulder or arm, use the improvisational curved piecing method, described here, to fill in these areas to form a block.

Improvisational curved piecing:
Layer a piece of shirting fabric, **Right**-side up, underneath the armhole section you wish to attach it to, and cut the underneath fabric to the line of the curve, leaving a ¼-in/6-mm overhang on the underneath piece for the seam allowance. Remember, the sharper the curve, the more difficult it will be to sew together; therefore, you may wish to widen the curve by trimming both the convex and concave pieces to match (see page 22 for more help on piecing curves).

To ensure accurate sewing, first line up the curved pieces next to each other, both with **Right** sides facing up, and mark registration lines across the concave and convex curves of the two fabrics with tailor's chalk. Then turn over the filler piece so that the **Right** sides are now facing, and match up the registration lines. Pin the center chalk lines first, and then ease the fabric between the pins as you continue to match up the registration marks and pin the remainder of the curve. Sew along this edge with a ¼-in/6-mm seam allowance. Press the seam in the direction it naturally falls.

To preserve the interesting necklines and collars:
Place a piece of shirting; with the **Right** side facing up, underneath the collar or neckline (also **Right**-side up) that you are featuring; this forms the background on which the feature pieces will be sewn.

Pin the collar or neckline into place and use an appliqué hand stitch (a slip stitch or blanket stitch, depending on the effect you want) or a simple zig-zag or blanket machine stitch along the edge of the neckline, to sew it down onto the background fabric. After stitching in place, turn it over and trim away the extra fabric from the **Wrong** side to reduce bulk, leaving a ¼-in/6-mm seam allowance.

MAKING BLOCKS

1. Use the methods previously described to make several blocks. For this keepsake quilt, there were seven blocks. One was the child's shirt front and collar; another block was the mother's shirt front and collar. Another block was composed of sections of shirting from both shirts, pieced with curved strips. An additional two blocks were created using the sleeves of the infant's shirt and the mother's shirt, preserving the fastenings and cuffs, and another two blocks were made using curved piecing to preserve the armhole shapes.

JOINING THE BLOCKS TOGETHER

1. After you have made several blocks (which are approximately square in shape), you will need to fit them together. It is useful to have set aside some of the unused fabric from both shirts to help with adjusting the size of the blocks, in order to fit the pieces of the puzzle together.

2. If you need a section to be longer, then sew an extra piece of fabric to the end; if you need it to be shorter, trim to size. Press the seams as you go. Let the coincidental shape of your sections and the visual flow of the pieces determine the direction of your pattern.

3. Start with the heart of the quilt and attach a section onto one side (sewing the **Right** sides together), pressing the seams. Trim to create a straight line, and then find another section that is the right size and attach to the other side of the heart section in the same way. This section will form the center row of your quilt. Sew three or four more sections together to form the top row, and do the same to form the bottom row. Press all seams and adjust the sizes of the rows by adding fabric or trimming it away, so that they fit together. Sew the three rows together; making sure the heart section is in the center row. Press.

FINISHING THE QUILT

1. When you are happy with your quilt top, press the entire quilt top and trim the edges. Make a quilt sandwich with your batting, backing fabric, and quilt top and baste together using your preferred method.

2. This quilt has been hand quilted, using a contrasting thread, with curved lines—imitating the curve at the heart of the quilt—but feel free to quilt as you desire.

3. Bind the quilt using binding made from leftover scraps of the shirting and baby's clothing material. If you don't have any left over or the material you used is not suitable for binding, then use any other binding of your choice. Bind the quilt using the instructions on page 41.

A drawing originally intended as a children's book illustration inspired Imagine. It is part of a series created around a one-word concept. This quilt mixes the fabrics and colors in unexpected ways, to go along with the theme of imagination.

Imagine

by Jude Hill

Finished size: 13 x 22 in/33 x 56 cm

Difficulty level: **TRICKY**

MATERIALS

Dark-blue and light-blue scraps

13-in/33-cm strip selvage or strip of torn edge for the water's edge

7-x-13-in/17-x-33-cm strip of dark-blue fabric for the night sky section

½ yd/46 cm muslin for foundation on all three sections

Mottled greens, purple, and pale yellow strips (optional)

13-in/33-cm square hand-dyed fabric for the friendly creature

Seven 5-in/12.5-cm square scraps, in rainbow colors, for letters

Brown, red, and yellow fabric scraps for appliqué details

13-x-22-in/33-x-56-cm piece sturdy cotton for backing

Pink, blue, and green embroidery floss in various shades, including variegated

2-x-13-in/5-x-33-cm strip blue batik or hand-dyed fabric for bottom border behind the word "Imagine"

Yellow-gold embroidery floss for sun spirals, sun, and moon

13-in/33-cm strip lace or vintage linen for sea foam

Two 1-x-14-in/2.5-x-35.5-cm and two 1-x-22-in/2.5-x-56-cm torn strips plaid for binding

13-x-22-in/33-x-56-cm piece muslin for lining (in place of batting; optional)

Cotton quilting thread

List continues next page

NOTES

Seam allowances are all ¼ in/6 mm.

Quilt weaving has a double thickness—the foundation plus the two layers created by the weaving process eliminates the need for batting.

The background uses recycled indigo cloth mixed with batiks and scraps of tie-dye and men's shirting. The friendly creature is made from hand-dyed fabric with a stencil design in faded paint. The water-line is made up of different elements, including fringed selvage and vintage napkin edge with embroidered waves to give the sea a bit of detail and surface interest. The top border of stars is made paper-chain style, giving it a child's arts-and-crafts feel. The letters were cut from different-colored fabrics and arranged like a rainbow, representing a story with a happy ending.

The day sky and water are made using quilt weaving, where strips of fabric are torn and woven together and then applied to a foundation, where they are then basted and quilted. The quilt weaving process is surprisingly quick and provides an interesting and varied texture background for the appliqué design elements.

The binding is a simple ragged strip binding; a torn strip of plaid fabric encases the edge from front to back, overlapping each side ½ in/12 mm. A simple running stitch tacks it in place.

DIFFICULTY

This quilt is constructed in sections and layers and includes a woven patchwork base, appliqué and embroidered details, some painting for special effect, and a ragged-edge binding. It is primarily hand stitched and will take some time and attention; it is a piece to be made with love and treasured.

CUTTING

1. Tear fabric strips in a variety of blues. Width can vary from ¾ in/2 cm to 1⅝ in/4 cm; use lighter blues for day sky and darker tones for the sea section. Tear enough strips for each of the sections and cut a piece of muslin the correct size for each of the sections:

Continued from page 157

EXTRAS

Waterproof fine-point marker or waterproof fabric pen

White textile paint and brushes

Handmade or bought star template for painting

Embroidery needles

Permanent marker

TEMPLATES

Friendly creature

Letters

Island, boat, sun, moon, and star

TECHNIQUES

Piecing: quilt weaving

Hand stitches: running stitch, whipstitch, slip stitch, backstitch, and split stitch

Decorative element: fabric painting

Appliqué: needle turn appliqué, and hand stitched raw edge appliqué

Quilting: hand quilting

Binding: raw edge binding

a. Sea section: 13 x 13½ in/33 x 34 cm

b. Day sky section: 6½ x 13 in/16.5 x 33 cm

c. Night sky section: 7 x 13 in/17 x 33 cm

2. If you like, you can also mix some mottled greens and purple strips with dark blue for the sea and some pale yellow strips with the light blues for the sky.

3. Using the templates for the creature and the arm, trace with waterproof fine-point marker onto your dyed fabric and cut out leaving ¼ in/6 mm seam allowance to turn under.

4. Using the letter templates (or your own font design), trace one letter on each of your seven different 5-in-/12.5-cm-square scraps, each a different color of the rainbow. Cut out, leaving ¼ in/6 mm seam allowance to turn under.

5. Trace and cut out the island template from brown fabric, the sailboat and sail from red (or any contrasting fabric) and the sun and the moon from various yellow fabrics, leaving ¼ in/6 mm seam allowance to turn under.

6. Cut one 13-x-22-in/33-x-56-cm piece of sturdy cotton for the backing fabric.

ASSEMBLING THE QUILT TOP

1. Taking the torn strips for the sky and sea, weave them, using the muslin as a base:

a. For each section, cut enough vertical strips to the correct length and lay them next to each other over the foundation base (the muslin

piece). Baste and then machine sew across the top edge of the piece to secure the vertical strips onto the foundation.

b. Cut enough horizontal strips to fit the width of the piece. Lift every second strip and pull upward and out of the way. Lay down a horizontal strip, and then place the vertical strips back into position. Then pick up the alternate strips and pull up and out of the way. Lay another strip and then place the vertical strips back into position. Continue until the foundation is covered. Pin or stitch baste at intersection points.

c. Trim each of the three sections to size and sew all the way around with a machine stitch. Then overlap the sea section onto the sky section by ½ in/12 mm, and machine stitch to attach.

d. Hand sew a running stitch through the center of each strip in both directions and then along the edges here and there; this secures the woven strips down in the center and doubles as quilting (additional quilting may be added later). Whipstitch has been added to the horizontal ragged edges to secure the surface and add color.

- -

MAKING THE CREATURE

1. Decorate your cut-out fabric creature with stars and dots, using watered-down white textile paint and a star stencil.

2. Arrange the creature onto the sea section, as shown on the diagram, and baste into place. Then appliqué the beast by turning the edges under up to the line, and sew into place using an invisible slip stitch. Arrange the arm of the beast into position and pin and sew as before.

3. Decorate the beast a little by outlining the arms with 3 strands of embroidery floss in backstitch. Paint on the eye and embroider around it with a split stitch. Embroider the cheek using a running stitch in variegated pink thread. Then outline the beast using variegated green or blue floss, with a split stitch or backstitch.

4. Draw water ripples over the sea section, going right over the beast but taking care to avoid the eye and face details. Use a permanent marker and then embroider with variegated blue floss using backstitch; then follow the lines of the waves with rows of running stitch quilting to your liking.

MAKING THE LETTERING

1. Place the strip of torn batik or tie-dye at the bottom of the sea section and stitch down using a rustic running stitch; this forms the ocean floor and grounds the quilt design.

2. Place the letters into position at the bottom of the quilt and pin into place. Appliqué the letters using needle turn technique by turning the edges under and stitching down with a slip stitch.

- -

COMPLETING THE DAY SKY SECTION

1. Position the island on top of the creature's head. Turn the edges under and stitch in place. Do the same for the sailboat, sail, moon, and sun.

2. Draw random spirals over the sky and within the sun and cover them with a split stitch, using yellow-gold embroidery thread.

3. Place the lace linen to cover the seam between the sea and sky sections. Stitch down by quilting with a chunky-style running stitch.

- -

ATTACHING THE NIGHT SKY

1. Sew the night sky section onto the top of the day sky, the **Right** sides together, by machine, and then fold in half over the top of the piece, like a wide seam binding. Tack in place on the back and press. If you are using a muslin lining then insert this before folding the top section over.

2. Make the fabric stars by folding a strip of fabric, accordion style, so there are five layers. This strip can be a single color, or you can make a multicolored strip by sewing 3-x-5-in/7.5-x-12.5-cm pieces of different-colored fabrics together. Press to hold the shape and draw a star on the top layer—making sure the points go over the edge where the folds are (see star template). Cut out the star, being careful not to cut through the folded edge. Open it up to reveal a row of five stars joined together.

3. Place the strip of stars, attached to each other paper-chain style, across the top of the night sky section, pin into position, and appliqué the strip of stars, leaving the edges raw, onto the background fabric, by sewing around the edges of the stars using a whipstitch or blanket stitch or other folksy stitch.

- -

FINISHING THE QUILT

1. Take your backing fabric piece and place it back-to-back with the quilt top and baste all around the outside. Bind the edges using the ragged strips you cut earlier—no need to fold the raw edges under, as the ragged edges will be left for a folksy, handmade feel. Fold the binding square at the corners and either machine sew or hand sew a simple running stitch along the edge, through all the layers at once. Add a hanging sleeve (see page 45) and a label to the back, and you are done. This quilt makes for a beautiful decorative wall-art piece.

Glossary of Terms

Amish quilt making

Quilts made by the Amish community, a religious group that shuns modern conveniences. These hand-quilted textiles are known for their dark solid fabrics with geometric designs and heavy hand quilting.

Appliqué

The application of a decorative design by cutting pieces of material and stitching them to a background fabric.

Asymmetrical design

A design in an irregular shape; the opposite of a symmetrical design.

Background fabric

The foundation fabric or pieced backdrop of a quilt; the place for adding more elements of design, such as appliqué pieces.

Backing fabric

The fabric that goes on the back of the quilt.

Backstitching or back tacking

Stitching backward over the previous stitches to strengthen and reinforce seams.

Base plate, stitch plate, or throat plate

The metal plate beneath a sewing machine's needle and presser foot, with an opening for the needle to pass through as it stitches.

Basting

A loose, temporary sewing stitch to hold layers of fabric together; basting can also be done with pins or basting spray.

Basting spray

Spray glue used to baste the quilt layers together without sewing.

Batting

The stuffing, or center, of a quilt, also known as "wadding," which gives the quilt warmth and thickness.

Bearding

Synthetic batting that works its way through the fabric to the top of the quilt.

Bias

The diagonal grain across the fabric, at a 45-degree angle to the selvage.

Bias binding

Strips of fabric cut on the bias, used to bind the raw edges of the quilt.

Binding

The finished edge of a quilt, where binding, either single or double fold, is sewn over the edges of the layers of the quilt; it gives the quilt strength.

Bleeding

Loss of color in the fabric when washed; the color spreads out of its designated area and dyes the fabric nearby.

Block

A section that is sewn together with other blocks, usually in a repeating pattern, to make the quilt top.

Bobbin

In a sewing machine, the small spool, located underneath the base or throat plate, that holds the lower thread.

Butted seam

Two strips of fabric that are tightly butted together without any overlay or spacing, then sewn over, usually with a zigzag stitch.

Chain piecing

A method of sewing quilt blocks together in a continuous line with a chain of stitches between each block.

Clipped corners

Small wedges taken out of the seam allowance at the corners to reduce bulk and aid in making a crisp corner when the quilt is turned **Right**-side out.

Concentric circles

Circles that share the same center point, but have a different diameter.

Continuous binding

A continuous length of binding strip with a minimum of joining seams.

Cotton duck

A heavy, plain, woven cotton fabric often called "canvas"; it comes in a range of weights suitable for various applications.

Crazy patchwork

A method of stitching irregular and random pieces of fabric onto a foundation fabric to form a quilt block; this is often enhanced with decorative stitching.

Deconstructed clothing

Clothing that is taken apart for the purpose of salvaging and repurposing the materials and main features.

Decorative embroidery stitch

A stitch with an ornamental rather than practical purpose.

Decorator-weight fabric

A heavyweight, sturdy fabric used for upholstery or drapery.

Diptych

A single work of art composed of two separate pieces that are displayed side by side.

Disappearing-ink pen

A fabric pen or marker, with ink that dissolves in the air or with the help of a dab of water. Water-soluble pens and fabric pens that come with a special eraser are also available.

Double-fold binding

Binding that, when folded over the edge of a quilt, has a double layer of fabric.

Easing

To adjust the lengths of fabric when pinning and sewing so they match up.

Echo quilting

To stitch quilting lines around a quilt block or appliqué motif that echo the shape; these lines then radiate out from the design in a concentric pattern.

Embroidery

Fancy stitch work and decorative designs, made with needle and thread onto fabric.

Embroidery floss

Thread that is made specifically for embroidery and other forms of needlework.

Embroidery or quilting hoop

A device used to keep fabric taut while hand stitching. It is made of two concentric wooden or plastic circles; the fabric is placed between the hoops and they are tightened with a screw to keep the fabric in place.

Emery pincushion

A small pincushion filled with emery, used to help keep needles and pins sharp. Emery is a very hard type of rock that when ground into a powder is used as an abrasive.

English paper piecing

A type of patchwork that involves using paper templates, which are basted onto fabric and then sewn together with a whipstitch rather than a running stitch.

Facing

An invisible binding or lining applied to the edge of a garment for strengthening and for finishing a raw edge.

Feed dogs

The metal teeth that emerge from a hole in the throat plate on a sewing machine. Their job is to grip the underside of the fabric and push it along.

Finger press

When you use your fingers to press a seam open rather than using an iron.

Foundation blocks

Sewing pieces of fabric onto a paper or a muslin foundation to form a quilt block. Used in crazy quilting and in foundation paper piecing.

Freeform quilting

Also known as "free-motion quilting," a technique in which the fabric is quilted using a rambling, all-over design.

Freezer paper

A heavy white paper with a plastic coating on one side, it is used in quilting or fabric stencils as a template, because it stays on fabric when ironed and is easily removed without leaving any residue.

Fusible batting

Batting that contains a fusible web on both sides; it is placed between the quilt top and quilt back and the glue is heat activated when the fabric is ironed.

Fusible web

A web-like material that fuses fabric pieces together when heat activated with a warm iron.

Gee's Bend quilters

Gee's Bend is a small rural community in Alabama, in which, over several generations, the town's women developed a unique quilting style characterized by geometric simplicity; these quilts are often made with recycled fabrics and utilize an improvised approach to design.

Gocco Screen Print

A self-contained printing system invented in 1977 in Japan.

Grain

The direction of the fabric, warp or weft. "With the grain" means parallel to the warp, or the length of the yardage.

Graphic prints

A term used to describe fabric that has a contrast of tone and uses text or illustrative elements.

Hand-dyed fabric

Fabric dyed by hand; it often has a mottled appearance where there are subtle differences in shade throughout.

Hand stitch or hand sew

To sew fabric with a needle and thread by hand as opposed to using a sewing machine.

Hanging sleeve

A sleeve or pouch attached to the back of the quilt, enabling it to be hung on the wall while retaining its original shape.

Improvisational piecing

A type of patchwork where no pattern is used; instead it is sewn as you go, using whatever fabric you have on hand.

Ink-jet fabric

Specially treated fabric made to go into an ink-jet printer.

Log cabin

A quilt block in which the center square is made first and rectangular "logs" are added around it, in sequence.

Meter or metre

Unit of measurement equal to 100 cm, 1.094 yards, or 39.4 inches.

Mitered corner

The corner of the binding around a quilt that is joined at a 45-degree angle.

Muslin

Plain, unbleached cotton, used as a neutral background, or as foundation fabric in quilting (also called "calico" in Australia and the United Kingdom).

Patchwork blocks

Pieced (sewn) squares consisting of repeated shapes to create patterns.

Pearl cotton or Perle cotton

An embroidery thread with a high sheen, sold in three sizes.

Piecing

Sewing pieces of fabric together to make patchwork.

Pillowcase method

Also called "envelope binding" or "bagging out"; a method of finishing a quilt in which the quilt edges are sewn inside out, leaving a small opening with which to then turn the quilt **Right**-side out.

Pin basting

A method of basting in which small safety pins are used to secure the layers of quilt together while you quilt.

"Pinch and turn" appliqué

Also called "needle turn" appliqué, a method used to sew the edges of the appliqué under as you sew rather than basting or ironing them in place beforehand.

Piping

A strip of fabric-covered cord used to edge hems.

Prairie points

Folded triangles of fabric used to add a decorative edge to quilts.

Presser foot

The part of the sewing machine that sits on the fabric, pressing it as you sew. Different types of presser feet do different jobs: A free-motion foot for free-motion sewing such as quilting or embroidery works effectively with the feed dogs in the down position; walking foot walks the top of the fabric at the same time as the feed dogs walk the bottom fabric and is used for sewing multiple layers of fabric.

Puckering

Folds or wrinkles in the fabric; these can occur when quilting and are not desirable.

Quilt sandwich

The three layers of the quilt—backing, batting, and decorative quilt top.

Raw edge appliqué

A technique in which the edge of the appliqué motif is not turned under but is instead sewn in place with the raw edge still showing.

Registration marks

Marks, lines, dots, or crosses placed on a pattern, ensuring accurate positioning.

Reverse appliqué

A technique in which the motif, instead of being sewn onto the quilt top or background fabric, is cut out of the top fabric to reveal a layer of fabric underneath.

Rotary cutter

A tool with a circular blade, used to cut fabric.

Sashiko stitch

A decorative running stitch where the stitches are placed at precise intervals, with a slightly longer stitch on the top than on the underside of the fabric.

Seam allowance

The space between the sewn seam and the edge of the fabric; it is usually ¼ in/6 mm in quilting.

Seam ripper

A tool for removing stitches.

Self-binding

A technique in which the backing fabric of the quilt is brought over to the front to act as a binding.

Selvage

Also spelled "selvedge," this is the long side edge of cloth that is reinforced to prevent unraveling.

"Sew and flip" technique

A method in which pieces of scrap fabric are sewn onto a foundation fabric; the fabric is sewn **Right**-side down along one edge, and then flipped over; further pieces are sewn over this piece until the whole foundation fabric is covered.

Sewing notions

Sewing tools and equipment.

Shibori

An ancient Japanese resist dye method.

Single-fold binding

Binding that is made with the edges turned in toward the center; only a single fold of fabric covers the raw edge of the quilt.

Square up

To ensure that the corners are 90 degrees and the edges are completely straight.

"Stitch in the ditch"

Quilting stitches that are made directly on top of the seams.

Straight-cut binding

Binding that is made with strips cut on the straight grain of the fabric.

Tacking

Also called "basting," this is a loose stitch used to temporarily hold layers of fabric together until they are stitched permanently.

Tension

A setting on the sewing machine that can be adjusted to ensure the stitches are even on the top and bottom of the fabric.

Topstitch

A straight stitch, used to give a crisp, defined edge.

Tying a quilt

Securing the quilt sandwich layers together by adding loose threads and then tying knots in them at intervals across the quilt.

Unbleached cotton

Cotton fabric that has not been treated with bleaching agents or dye, it is often an off-white or beige color.

Yard

A unit of length that equals 3 feet or 91.44 cm.

Sewing and Quilting Resources Guide

BOOKS

Books always inspire me. Nothing beats the feeling of picking up a book to read and ponder while you think up your next project. Here are some of the books I recommend for quilting tips and ideas:

The American Quilt: A History of Cloth and Comfort 1750–1950. Roderick Kiracofe and Mary Elizabeth Johnson. Clarkson Potter (2004): If you are interested in quilting history, then this is a must-have—it has gorgeous photos and is an interesting read.

The Art of Manipulating Fabric. Colette Wolff. Chilton Book Company (1996): Invaluable source of sewing techniques.

The Complete Encyclopedia of Needlework. Therese De Dillmont (1884): Even though it is more than one hundred years old, it is still relevant today—it contains many sewing basics. (This is an open source book and is available for download from www.gutenberg.org/ebooks/20776.)

Denyse Schmidt Quilts: 30 Colorful Quilt and Patchwork Projects. Denyse Schmidt. Chronicle Books (2005): Simple and elegant designs for beginner quilters.

Encyclopedia of Pieced Quilt Patterns. Barbara Brackman. American Quilter's Society (1993): Reference guide for identifying quilt designs.

Encyclopedia of Sewing Machine Techniques. Nancy Bednar and JoAnn Pugh-Gannon. Sterling (2007): Indispensable for information on how to get the most out of your sewing machine.

The History of the Patchwork Quilt: Origins, Traditions and Symbols of a Textile Art. Schnuppe Von Gwinner. Schiffer Publishing (1988): For the history of quilting beyond American folk-art traditions.

Lotta Prints: How to Print with Anything, from Potatoes to Linoleum. Lotta Jansdotter. Chronicle Books (2008): A great resource guide for simple printing techniques.

The Modern Quilt Workshop: Patterns, Techniques, and Designs from the Funquilts Studio. Bill Kerr and Weeks Ringle. Quarry Books (2005): A wealth of quilting information, great tips, and modern designs.

Quilter's Complete Guide. Marianne Fons and Liz Porter. Oxmoor House (2001): A must-have book for beginner quilters.

The Quilts of Gee's Bend: Masterpieces from a Lost Place. William Arnett, Alvia Wardlaw, Jane Livingston, and John Beardsley. Tinwood Books (2002): Fantastic inspiration, gorgeous quilts.

Shibori: A Beginner's Guide to Creating Color and Texture on Fabric. Lynne Caldwell. Lark Books (2006): An excellent guide to Shibori basics.

Shibori: The Inventive Art of Japanese Shaped Resist Dyeing. Yoshiko Iwamoto Wada, Mary Kellogg Rice, and Jane J. Barton. Kodansha International (1999): An essential, in-depth book on all types of Shibori.

Spotless: Room-by-Room Solutions to Domestic Disasters. Shannon Lush and Jennifer Fleming. Ebury Press (2008). A fantastic guide to cleaning and caring for your fabrics (and other household goods) the natural way without resorting to chemicals.

The Uncommon Quilter: Small Art Quilts Created with Paper, Plastic, Fiber, and Surface Design. Jeanne Williamson. Potter Craft (2007): Great inspiration for experimental quilt design.

SEWING, FABRIC, AND QUILTING ONLINE RESOURCES

SEWING, QUILTING AND CRAFTY BLOGS

angrychicken.typepad.com
Sewing and quilting blog

annamariahorner.blogspot.com
Fabric designer with sewing, quilting, and design tips

aquiltisnice.blogspot.com
Quilting blog with tips and tutorials

crazymomquilts.blogspot.com
Tutorials and quilting tips

handmadebyalissa.com
Quilting blog with tips and tutorials

heatherbailey.typepad.com
Sewing, design, and fabric tips

houseonhillroad.typepad.com/my_weblog
Sewing tips and tutorials

mayamade.blogspot.com
Lots of sewing and crafty tutorials

meetmeatmikes.blogspot.com
Australian crafty Web site

mollychicken.blogs.com
UK sewing and craft blog

nikkishell.typepad.com
Australian sewing blog—dedicated to refashioning (i.e. repurposing and reusing materials for clothing and natural living

ohfransson.com
Quilting tips and tutorials

www.quiltersbuzz.com
The latest in quilting and fabric news

sewmamasew.com/blog2/
Sewing tutorials and fabric shop

thimble.ca
Canadian sewing and craft blog

treefalldesign.typepad.com
UK sewing and craft blog

www.trueup.net
Fabric addiction

whipup.net
Handcraft in a hectic world

yarnstorm.blogs.com
UK-based craft blog

SEWING AND QUILTING ONLINE RESOURCES AND MAGAZINES

amybutlerdesign.com
Fabric designer and free online patterns

burdastyle.com
Open source sewing

craftster.org
The essential crafty forum

www.duquilts.com.au
Down Under Quilts—Australian quilting magazine with a free digital subscription

livingcreatively.com.au
Australian online craft magazine

www.quiltindex.org
Research and reference tool with images and information about quilts held in private and public hands in America

www.quilting.about.com
General quilting reference and resource site.

www.quiltstudy.org
International quilt study center and museum

suzical.co.uk/sewing-blogs.html
Check out the big list of sewing blogs

Flickr is a fantastic photo-sharing Web site that designers and makers use to share their creations. There are many quilting groups to join:

www.flickr.com/groups/386698@N23/
Doll quilt crazy

www.flickr.com/groups/dollquiltswap/pool/
Doll quilt swap

www.flickr.com/groups/embroideredstuff/pool
Flickr embroidery group

ONLINE COLOR TOOLS

These Web sites create a color palette from an uploaded photo.

www.bighugelabs.com

www.colorblender.com

www.colorhunter.com

www.colr.org

www.degraeve.com/color-palette

www.genopal.com/online

SOME FUN ONLINE DESIGN TOOLS

I love this open-source online program; it generates nine-patch patchwork blocks for you.

levitated.net/daily/lev9block.html

Explore color, shape, and design with these open source tools:

levitated.net/daily/levGoldenSpiral.html

levitated.net/daily/levPantonGeo.html

levitated.net/daily/levQuarterRound.html

WHERE TO BUY TOOLS, SUPPLIES, AND FABRIC

amitie.com.au
Australian fabric and quilting store

cottonpatch.co.uk
UK online fabric and haberdashery store

duckcloth.com.au
Australian online fabric store selling the work of independent fabric designers

equilter.com
Online fabric store with a massive range of fabrics

www.etsy.com
Easily searchable marketplace where you can find just about any crafting material or handmade object

hempfabric.co.uk
Online resource for organic cotton, hemp, and bamboo fabric

inkandspindle.blogspot.com
Independent fabric design studio in Australia

kelanifabric.com.au
Australian online fabric store

kimoyes.com.au
Australian source for vintage Japanese fabric

kleins.co.uk
UK online haberdashery store

modern-craft.net
Japanese fabric and supplies

patchworkoncentralpark.com.au
Australian online fabric store

pinkchalkfabrics.com
Fabric, patterns, and tutorials

printscharming.com.au
Australian fabric designers

prochemical.com
Online store for fabric dye supplies

purlbee.com
Sewing, quilting, and other crafts

www.reprodepot.com
Great range of retro and hard-to-find fabrics

www.retrosaria.rosapomar.com
Portuguese fabrics

sewtrue.com
Online sewing supply store

www.spoonflower.com
Design your own fabric online and have it printed on demand

www.superbuzzy.com
Japanese fabric and supplies

valdani.com
Online haberdashery and quilting supply store

www.volksfaden.de
Online fabric store based in Europe

Designer Bios

Alison Brookbanks

Concentric Circles { page 114 }

Alison Brookbanks approaches her designs as a means of manipulating texture, touch, color, and shape. She draws on all elements of design and allows an architectural feel to come through in her pieces, echoing her profession as an architect. She likes to work on projects in which the creative process is an integral part of the final piece. Alison lives in Sydney, Australia, and you can find her online at **www.sixandahalfstitches.typepad.com**.

Lisa Call

Modern Geometric Quilt { page 124 }

Self-confessed "geek artist" **Lisa Call** is a full-time software engineer, single mom, and contemporary quilter. Her work is abstract but draws elements from many sources: colors, geology, repetition, pattern, and man-made structures. Lisa began making quilts in 1993 and her work has been included at Quilt National (even appearing on the 2003 Exhibition Catalog cover), as well as in numerous solo shows around the country. Lisa lives in Denver, Colorado, and can be found online at **www.lisacall.com**.

Boo Davis

Two Heads Are Better than One { page 146 }

Boo Davis is a designer, illustrator, and quilt maker working under the business name Quiltsrÿche. She spent much of her youth cozied up under her grandmother's quilt listening to Ozzy. As a grown-up metalhead and design geek, she finds the intersection of cute and evil to be most compelling. Applying a heavy-metal spin to the traditional craft of quilting seemed like a natural merging of her two great loves. Boo lives in Seattle, Washington, and can be found online at **www.quiltsryche.com**.

Malka Dubrawsky

English Flower Garden Quilt { page 52 }

Malka Dubrawsky grew up watching her mother sew and knit, but it wasn't until she was at home with her own children that she began working with textiles. She went on to combine her printmaking background with a career in fiber art, and her work has been exhibited at Quilt National. Recently she has been working on making functional textiles with her hand-dyed fabric, inspired by patterns in nature and architecture. She loves knowing that the hands of others will touch her work. Malka lives in Austin, Texas, and you can find her online at **www.stitchindye.blogspot.com**.

Victoria Gertenbach

Grasshopper in My Garden { page 90 }

Victoria Gertenbach has been intrigued by textiles from the time she was a little girl, playing on the floor with leftover fabric scraps from her mother's sewing projects. She is fascinated by the small details—the little and the overlooked. She delights in knowing that tiny worlds are all around us, and what sparks her imagination can be completely different from day to day. Victoria lives in Lancaster, Pennsylvania, and can be found online at **www.thesillyboodilly.blogspot.com** and **www.sillyboodilly.etsy.com**.

Lizette Greco + Grecolaborativo

T-R-E-G-R-! Map Quilt { page 66 }

The works of **Lizette Greco + Grecolaborativo** are the product of a full family collaboration—a couple creating with their two young children. They base their plush art on the children's drawings and make them with recycled materials. They aim to create artwork that celebrates a child's perspective of the world and will hopefully be passed from generation to generation. Lizette, originally from Chile, now lives in California with her family and can be found online at **www.lizettegreco.com**.

Liz Harvatine

1984 ("Pegasus Rainbow") Quilt { page 136 }

Liz Harvatine works with her husband as a stop-motion animator. She has bachelor's degrees in math and computer science and is obsessed with crafting of all kinds, most recently quilting. Liz lives in Los Angeles, California, and can be found online at **www.ladyharvatine.com**.

Jude Hill

Imagine { page 156 }

Jude Hill has always loved drawing and making things from fabric. Her upbringing in a do-it-yourself family led her to realize her sketches, first as doll clothes then as her own clothes. After studying children's book illustration, she went on to study woven fabric design, discovering the meditative benefits of hand quilting while commuting to work each day. Now Jude uses mostly recycled materials in her work and is primarily "unplugged" (hand sewing all her quilts). She wants her work to tell a story, and she is inspired by folk and ethnic textiles, as well as recycling and "slow" cloth. She lives in Centerport, New York, and can be found online at **www.spiritcloth.typepad.com**.

Lucinda Jones

Blackbird at My Window ("Cheeky Blackbird") { page 86 }

Lucinda Jones is a horticulturist living in a restored farmhouse. She has been sewing since childhood. She combines her love of gardening and the countryside with her sewing skills to create whimsical nature-inspired quilts. Lucinda lives in Morrisville, New York, and can be found online at **www.septemberbird.wordpress.com**.

Shannon Lamden

Cheater's ("Aunty Cookie") Quilt { page 120 }

Shannon Lamden is a fabric designer. All the fabrics used in the Cheater's Quilt are her own designs. Shannon draws or creates something every day; if she doesn't, she gets quite tetchy. When she is creating, she is in her happy place, completely relaxed and calm. She enjoys nothing more than a nice cup of tea, a speedy Internet connection, making and drawing, and hanging out with her family. Shannon lives in Melbourne, Australia, and can be found online at **www.auntycookie.com**.

Kristine Lempriere

Road Transport Quilted Pillow { page 76 }

Kristine Lempriere has been crafting since age four, when her grandmother taught her to crochet. She has always loved fabric and sewing and for the last seven years she has been running her own children's wear business, Townmouse. Her three boys are her current inspiration for machine appliquéd quilts with boy-related themes, but she is also enormously inspired by traditional and vintage quilts and crafting methods. Kristine lives in Melbourne, Australia, and she can be found online at **www.townmouse.com.au**.

Alix McAlister

Circus Quilt { page 70 }

Alix McAlister's life is one big patchwork. Having worked and lived in many different situations, she now tries to keep her life sewn together with a purpose. She secretly aspires to become a storyteller with a large quilt spread over her lap, inviting the audience to choose a patch of fabric and from there telling its story. She has collected and hoarded fabric for years but only began sewing after becoming a mother a few years ago. Alix lives in London, England. You can find her online at **www.fidalix.blogspot.com**.

Alicia Paulson

Pensive Pansy Photo Quilt { page 48 }

A craft designer and author, **Alicia Paulson** grew up in a creative family and at age thirteen was already running her first "business," where she sold handmade model-horse blankets through a classified ad in a magazine. She now works from her home studio, selling her "handmades" through her online store. She's the author of *Stitched in Time: Memory-Keeping Projects to Sew and Share*. She lives in Portland, Oregon, and you can find her online at **www.AliciaPaulson.com**.

Alexandra Rasmussen

Blattwerk { page 106 }

Living in ever-so-busy Yokohama, Japan, German-born **Alexandra Rasmussen** finds serenity in crafting and takes inspiration from the local streets. She loves color, texture, and working with natural materials, often repurposing used items or found objects. Alexandra can be found online at **www.moonstitches.typepad.com**.

Kathreen Ricketson

Shibori Sampler { page 102 }

Kathreen Ricketson is a mother, wife, and maker. She works part-time as a designer and is the founding editor of WhipUp.net. In her spare time she sews and is slightly addicted to fabric of all sorts (her secret vice is searching out vintage materials). She lives in Canberra, Australia, with her husband and two children and can be found online at **www.whipup.net**.

Ruth Singer

Constellations Quilt { page 128 }

Ruth Singer, an artist who has a background in museums and costume making, creates unique textile pieces that lean toward the tactile, using traditional techniques such as pleating, gathering, and quilting to create unusual textures and surface decoration. Ruth is the author of *Sew It Up*, and lives in Leicester, England. She can be found online at **www.ruthsinger.com** and **www.mantua-maker.blogspot.com**

Lisa Solomon

Target Pillow { page 142 }

Lisa Solomon grew up sewing, learning from her grandmother, and then designing costumes in college. She now uses these skills in her art practice. Her work revolves around themes of domesticity and gender, often using traditionally feminine craft skills to alter or repurpose the original meaning of found objects. Lisa's work reclaims time-honored techniques; as she looks to the past for inspiration, blending the old with the new, she questions the compatibility of art and craft. Lisa lives in Oakland, California. Find her online at **www.lisasolomon.com**.

Meg Spaeth

Power-line Sky { page 110 }

Meg Spaeth didn't grow up in a particularly crafty household; her family's creativity lay in the appreciation of books and preparation of food. After Meg graduated with a degree in philosophy, she turned to cooking, first as a baker then a chocolatier. After she became a mother, her creativity took a new direction, and, thanks to her supportive friends and family and the vibrant online craft scene, she has learned to sew and has been inspired to keep on sewing. Meg lives in Madison, Wisconsin, and can be found online at **www.elsiemarley.com**.

Sarah Steedman

Warbler Quilt { page 82 }

Sarah Steedman's work is influenced by her love of nature and art, having studied arts and agricultural ecology in college. After having a baby, she was inspired to make stuffed animals out of recycled sweaters and fabric, which soon turned into a full-time business, Scrappynation. She is constantly keeping her hands busy making something with fabric or yarn. Sarah lives in Chicago, Illinois, and can be found online at **www.scrappynation.com.**

Nicole Vaughan

Granny's Delight { page 132 }

Nicole Vaughan started crafting in her thirties. She always knew she needed a crafty outlet—it just took her a while to figure it out. After a friend introduced her to knitting, she quickly discovered that she has a serious craft addiction. She now flits between embroidery, knitting, sewing, crochet, jewelry making, screen printing, and more. Blogging fuels her craft obsessions and has connected her with like-minded people across the world. Nicole lives in Perth, Australia, with her partner and pets. She's a regular contributor to www.whipup.net and the cocreator of backtack.blogspot.com. Her crafting adventures can be followed at **www.craftapalooza.typepad.com.**

Betz White

Loopy Quilt { page 62 }

Betz White is a designer, author, and eco-crafter who combines her whimsical color and design sense with a love for repurposing. Five years ago, Betz left her former career as a children's wear designer to pursue her love of crafting. She is the author of *Sewing Green*. Betz lives in North Potomac, Maryland, and can be found online at **www.betzwhite.com.**

Kajsa Wikman

Follow Your Heart Art Quilt { page 56 }

An ethnologist, **Kajsa Wikman** is influenced by vintage textiles. In her fiber work, traditional materials and techniques meet contemporary ideas, inspired by her two children and folk art. Kajsa crafts because she can share joy through her handmade objects and feels like she is doing her share against mass consumerism by making "slow" hand-crafted things. Kajsa lives in Helsinki, Finland, and can be found online at **www.sykossa.blogspot.com.**

Sherri-Lynn Wood

Keepsake Quilt { page 152 }

Sherri-Lynn Wood is an artist, activist, and healer. She combines her knowledge of craft, sculpture, and theology to create contexts for social exchange that reacquaint people with personal agency, community, care, love, and the basic skills of living. Sherri began Passage Quilts in 2001, an active bereavement and transition process, utilizing the clothing of the deceased and materials of life. Sherri lives in San Francisco, California, and can be found online at **www.passagequilts.com.**

Kellie Wulfsohn

A Little Birdie Told Me { page 96 }

Kellie Wulfsohn has always had a love of art and enjoyed creating. However, it wasn't until after the birth of her twins that she discovered her obsession with fabric, and she now designs and makes appliqué quilts. She believes that anything is possible given enough time and determination, and this is how she goes about most things in her life, including her design process. Kellie lives in Melbourne, Australia, with her four children and husband. She can be found online at **www.dontlooknow.typepad.com.**

Index

A

Adhesive, paper-backed, 19, 24-25
Appliqué, 8-9, 23-25

B

Backing, 33
Backstitch, 30
Bagging out, 41
Basting, 34-35
Batting, 33-34
Beeswax, 16
Bias tape maker, 17
Binding, 39-44
Blackbird at My Window
    ("Cheeky Blackbird"), 86-89
Blanket stitch, 29
Blattwerk, 106-9
Blind stitch, 29
Blogs, 167
Bobbins, 15
Books, 166-67
Brookbanks, Alison, 115, 170

C

Call, Lisa, 125, 170
Carbon paper, 17
Chain piecing, 23
Chain stitch, 30
Cheater's ("Aunty Cookie")
    Quilt, 120-23
Circus Quilt, 70-75
Color, 11, 168
Concentric Circles, 114-18
Constellations Quilt, 128-30
Corners, mitered, 41
Craft knives, 17
Cross-stitch, 30
Curved piecing, 22
Cutting mats, 18

D

Davis, Boo, 147, 170
Design tools, online, 168
Design walls, 17
Dubrawsky, Malka, 53, 170

E

Embroidery hoops, 17
English Flower Garden Quilt, 52-55
English paper piecing, 21
Envelope method, 41

F

Fabric
    buying, 11, 169
    color of, 11
    dyeing, 26-28
    pressing, 12-13
    selecting, 11
    storing, 12
    vintage, 12
    washing, 12
Fabric glue, 18
Fabric markers, 17
Fabric paint, 18
Facing, 42-43
Feed dogs, 15
Flower Garden Quilt, English, 52-55
Follow Your Heart Art Quilt, 56-60
Four-patch design, 21
Fray-check spray, 19
Free-motion (freestyle) quilting, 37-38
Freezer paper, 18, 24
French knot, 31

G

Gertenbach, Victoria, 91, 170
Granny's Delight, 132-35
Grasshopper in My Garden, 90-95
Greco, Lizette, 67, 170

H

Hanging sleeves, 45
Harvatine, Liz, 137, 171
Hill, Jude, 157, 171

I

Imagine, 156-61
Improvisational piecing, 22
Interfacing, fusible, 19
Invisible slip stitch, 29
Irons, 16

J

Jones, Lucinda, 87, 171

K

Keepsake Quilt, 152-55

L

Lamden, Shannon, 121, 171
Laundry starch, 19
Leather punches, 17
Lempriere, Kristine, 77, 171
Lighting, 15
A Little Birdie Told Me, 96-100
Log cabin design, 21
Loopy Quilt, 62-65

M

Masking tape, 18
McAlister, Alix, 71, 171
Modern Geometric Quilt, 124-27

N

Needles, 15, 16, 36
Needle turn method, 24
Nine-patch design, 20
1984 ("Pegasus Rainbow") Quilt, 136-41

O

Online resources, 167-68

P

Paulson, Alicia, 49, 172
Pensive Pansy Photo Quilt, 48-51
Piecing, 21-23
Pillowcase method, 41-42
Pillows
    Road Transport Quilted
        Pillow, 76-80
    Target Pillow, 142-45
Pinch and turn method, 24
Pincushion, 16
Pins, 16
Piping, 44
Power-line Sky, 110-13
Prairie points, 43
Presser feet, 14

Q

Quilt blocks, 20-21
Quilting
    definition of, 36
    free-motion (freestyle), 37-38
    hand, 36-37
    machine, 37-38
    preparing for, 33-35
    straight, 37, 38
Quilting gloves, 18
Quilting rulers, 17
Quilts (general)
    binding, 39-44
    elements of, 33-34
    facing, 42-43
    hanging, 45
    history of, 8-10
    labeling, 46
    signing, 46
    small, 7-8
    storing, 46
    washing, 46
Quilts (specific)
    Blackbird at My Window
        ("Cheeky Blackbird"), 86-89
    Blattwerk, 106-9
    Cheater's ("Aunty Cookie")
        Quilt, 120-23
    Circus Quilt, 70-75
    Concentric Circles, 114-18
    Constellations Quilt, 128-30
    English Flower Garden
        Quilt, 52-55
    Follow Your Heart Art Quilt, 56-60
    Granny's Delight, 132-35
    Grasshopper in My Garden, 90-95
    Imagine, 156-61
    Keepsake Quilt, 152-55
    A Little Birdie Told Me, 96-100
    Loopy Quilt, 62-65
    Modern Geometric Quilt, 124-27
    1984 ("Pegasus Rainbow")
        Quilt, 136-41
    Pensive Pansy Photo Quilt, 48-51
    Power-line Sky, 110-13
    Road Transport Quilted
        Pillow, 76-80
    Shibori Sampler, 102-5
    Target Pillow, 142-45
    T-R-E-G-R-! Map Quilt, 66-69
    Two Heads Are Better than
        One, 146-50
    Warbler Quilt, 82-85
Quilt top
    definition of, 20, 33
    making, 20-23

R

Rasmussen, Alexandra, 107, 172
Reverse appliqué, 25
Ricketson, Kathreen, 103, 172
Road Transport Quilted Pillow, 76-80
Rotary cutters, 18
Running stitch, 29-30

S

Safety pins, 18, 34
Satin stitch, 31
Scissors, 16
Seam rippers, 16
Seams, pressing, 12-13
Self-binding, 43
Sewing kits, 19
Sewing machines, 14-15
Shibori dyeing, 27-28
Shibori Sampler, 102-5
Singer, Ruth, 129, 172
Slip stitch, 29
Solomon, Lisa, 143, 172
Spaeth, Meg, 111, 172
Split stitch, 31
Spray basting, 19, 34-35
Stabilizer, 19
Steedman, Sarah, 83, 173
Stem stitch, 31-32
Stenciling, 26
Stitches
    back-, 30
    blanket, 29
    blind, 29
    chain, 30
    cross-, 30
    French knot, 31
    running, 29-30
    satin, 31
    slip, 29
    split, 31
    stem, 31-32
    straight, 32
    tacking, 34
    whip-, 30
Storage ideas, 19, 46
Straight quilting, 37, 38
Straight stitch, 32
Supplies
    buying, 169
    storing, 19

T

Tacking stitches, 34
Tailor's chalk, 17
Tape measures, 16
Target Pillow, 142-45
Tea dyeing, 27
Tension check, 15
Thimbles, 18
Thread, 15
Tools, 14-19, 169
Tracing paper, 18
Transfer pencils, 19
T-R-E-G-R-! Map Quilt, 66-69
Two Heads Are Better than One, 146-50

V

Vaughan, Nicole, 133, 173

W

Warbler Quilt, 82-85
Web, fusible, 19, 24-25
Whipstitch, 30
White, Betz, 63, 173
Wikman, Kajsa, 57, 173
Wood, Sherri-Lynn, 153, 173
Wulfsohn, Kellie, 97, 173

Acknowledgments

I would like to dedicate this book to my two children, Otilija and Orlando. They are my constant source of inspiration: they continually help me reevaluate what is important in life and give me reason to create.

Many thanks to the wonderful designers, artists, and makers who have contributed designs to this book; these women juggle family, work, and life and still find time for a sewing project. Thank you for trusting me with your designs.

Very special thanks to my incredibly supportive husband, Rob, who takes an active interest in my projects and encourages me when I only have a spark of an idea. He is also the technical guru (along with my little brother, Jonathan) and behind-the-scenes dude for WhipUp.net, and he went beyond the call of duty to deliver more than one hundred illustrations for this book. Thank you for being nice even when I am not.

Thanks to my agent Courtney Miller-Callihan—this book would not have happened without you. Thank you to Jodi Warshaw and her colleagues at Chronicle Books for giving me this opportunity. Thank you to Amy Butler and Westminster Fibers for donating fabric. Thanks to my mother-in-law, Dace Shugg, for all her manuscript reading and pattern testing. Thanks also to my family: my parents, Warren and Janette, and brothers, Jonathan and Bruce, for showing me the everyday value of making things; my daughter, Otilija, who although only nine years old already has a very strong sense of style and a desire to create; and my son, Orlando, an everyday joy and inspiration.

Finally, a very special thank-you to the readers and contributors of WhipUp.net, who inspire me every day. And an especially big hug goes out to Nicole Vaughan, who has stuck it out with WhipUp.net from the very beginning.